THE DEATH & RESURRECTION

OF THE CHURCH

The
DEATH & RESURRECTION
of the CHURCH

Rustin E. Brian

FOREWORD BY
Derrick Thames

CASCADE *Books* · Eugene, Oregon

THE DEATH AND RESURRECTION OF THE CHURCH

Cascade Books
An Imprint of Wipf and Stock Publishers
199 W. 8th Ave., Suite 3
Eugene, OR 97401

www.wipfandstock.com

PAPERBACK ISBN: 978-1-7252-5155-7
HARDCOVER ISBN: 978-1-7252-5156-4
EBOOK ISBN: 978-1-7252-5157-1

Cataloguing-in-Publication data:

Names: Rustin, Brian E., author. Thames, Derrick, foreword.

Title: The death and resurrection of the church / Rustin E. Brian. Foreword
by Derrick Thames.

Description: Eugene, OR: Cascade Books, 2021 | Includes bibliographical
references.

Identifiers: ISBN 978-1-7252-5155-7 (paperback) | ISBN 978-1-7252-5156-4
(hardcover) | ISBN 978-1-7252-5157-1 (ebook)

Subjects: LCSH: Missions. | Christianity and culture. | Cultural pluralism—
Religious aspects—Christianity. | Church renewal.

Classification: BV2063 B71 2021 (print) | BV2063 (ebook)

To my children: Lily, Rowan, and Daisy. I pray that you will be good people, great friends, and that you will love God. May the church you encounter as you grow older be one filled with resurrection, and may you each, in turn, live out this resurrection life in and for the world.

TABLE OF CONTENTS

FOREWORD

TUESDAY THE 14TH OF August, 2018, is a day I will not soon forget because it was the day I first met Andrew. Two months prior, my wife, Dayna, and I, along with our three children, left Glasgow and the beautiful community church where I had pastored for seven years to start a new business and plant a new church in Dundee, Scotland. We did not simply leave Glasgow though, we were sent. In the UK, we have been grappling with the death of the church for a while now, and it still feels like we are behind. Many do not want to face the kind of stark reality that Rusty lays out so well in this book. Yet on our wee island, the facts are inescapable. The church is dying and is dead in many places. We don't talk about attendance percentages anymore. We know they are really bad! But we also know they are incapable of fully telling the stories of resurrection we see around us. We talk about living like we have got nothing to lose because the truth is we do not have anything to lose. We are like the football (soccer) team that is tied at the end of the game and sends their goalie up the pitch for a corner kick in hopes of something miraculous. Desperate times require desperate measures, right? So, when we told our church in Glasgow that God was calling us to leave the safety net of traditional pastoral ministry to start a coffee shop and plant a church in a new city where we did not know anyone, they were quick to get behind us. They knew this was necessary. The last new church to be planted in our particular tradition in Scotland was over twenty years ago. To my knowledge this is a similar situation in many other traditions in the UK! Throughout our going, I felt a bit like Tom Cruise in the movie *Jerry Maguire* as he left the large institution of Sports Agency with nothing more than a goldfish, Dorothy Boyd (Renée Zellweger) and a dream to spend more time with fewer clients.

Now back to that August morning when I first met Andrew. He was the first person I interviewed for a job in the coffee shop. Under normal circumstances, the interview would have ended before it got off the ground. Andrew was late, visibly anxious, avoided eye contact, and was unable to answer my questions with anything more than a "yes" or a "no." However, before the interview, he had explained via email how he struggled with depression and social anxiety and that he was reeling after the loss of his mother only six weeks prior. As I sat there wondering how this young man was going to cope in a busy coffee shop, something deep within me knew I had to give Andrew the job. I would come to discover that he actually left school four years prior to our meeting to become the sole caregiver for both of his sick parents. Andrew had no work experience, no confidence, barely spoke in public and hated coffee! He was not fit for the job, but he was exactly why we followed Jesus to Dundee. Andrew was a tiny spark of hope that perhaps all things could be made new.

Blend Coffee Lounge was born out of the death of the church, or at least a certain kind of church. The other seven adults and four children who moved with our family to Dundee did so because we were done with church as production and consumption. We were done with the church that had learned the language of the gospel without embodying its life. We were done with the church whose politics looked just like the power-grabbing, hierarchical structures of the world around us. But mostly, we were convinced that the church's goal is what Rusty calls faithfulness. We were convinced that we did not just have a message to proclaim but a message to live. And that, in fact, we are that message! We realized, to borrow Rusty's organic imagery, that the soil, the seed, and the surroundings had been contaminated, and the result was a malnourished, immature, and impatient church.

As a parent, arguably the most important role I play in the life of my children is to prepare them to be able to leave home, enter the world, and live as faithful witnesses of the gospel. If I do not prepare them to leave home and flourish by filling the earth with goodness and love, then I have failed at the single most important job I have as a parent. If my children cannot wash their clothes, cook good food, steward their money, be concerned about their neighbor, welcome the stranger, work honestly, turn the other cheek, practice forgiveness, speak truth, know where to look for wisdom, and navigate their surroundings in ways that honor Jesus, then I have not done my job. In a similar way, the Western church has too often failed to launch its people into the mission of God. We have not prepared our people to leave home, so to speak. We have gotten too comfortable being entertained in our large buildings with big screen TVs and large staff employed to make the Christian life convenient by producing user-friendly programs that protect the brand at all costs. In essence, we have failed in our single most important job as pastors and leaders.

So why start a coffee shop? Part of the beauty of the church is that each generation has to consider afresh what it means to be the people of God today—in this place. Hence, the value of the book you are holding in your hands! No generation has ever gotten it just right so as to leave us all a blueprint. Nor do we live in a static world. Maybe more than all of that is the fact that we are creative beings made in the image of God and filled with the Spirit of God to fill the earth with the good news of resurrection in Jesus Christ. Blend is what Rusty defines as a small-batch business. We started Blend to honor every person who walks through the door and to serve them the very best coffee available. Blend is neither a "Christian coffee shop," if there is such a thing, nor are we a church per se. However, as the church moves through death into resurrection, as Rusty says, we must be willing to "do" church differently, and Blend has become something of a different way to "do" church in the midst of the marketplace—a fresh expression of the goodness of God at the center of culture.

In 2012, I attended a special event with Alan Hirsch and Mike Frost hosted at what was then the International Christian College in Glasgow. They were talking about their seminal missional

work, *The Shaping of Things to Come*. There, I heard Mike explain
the missional practices found in the acronym he tries to live by:
BELLS. Or, bless, eat, listen, learn, and send. He has since written a book, *Surprise the World*, where he explains the profound
impact such practices can have upon the world around us. I was
moved by how simple and profound these missional practices
were and began to personalize them until I arrived at the acronym
of BLEND: bless, listen, eat, nurture and dare. Blend began as missional practices that our church in Glasgow began working out together until it eventually turned into the name of our small-batch,
missional business. Everyone who works for Blend must commit
to practicing these values. We call it "blending", and it is a part of
everyone's contract. These values are what have made us successful
over the past seven years in three very different cities. In this way,
Blend has provided the opportunity to create the environment for
what Rusty calls "small-batch church"—I love this term! It enables
employment not just for friends like Andrew, but also pastors like
myself who are enabled to support their families without burden-
ing a fledgling church. It also provides the avenue to move into the
neighborhood, provide a cultural good and serve our local community, one person at a time. Blend has also opened the door to a
world that we never had access to before. Now we can embody the
"hokey religion" of resurrection and renewal that Rusty refers to in
the heart of a marketplace culture.

In his book *The Church as the People of* God, Hans Kung said,
"A church which pitches its tents without constantly looking out
for new horizons, which does not continually strike camp, is being
untrue to its calling. . . . [We must] play down our longing for
certainty, accept what is risky, live by improvisation and experiment." We experimented with planting a small-batch church by
first starting a small-batch business, and so far it is working. We
are able to demonstrate to our staff/friends like Andrew what it is
to flourish in work and life by constantly pointing to Jesus. The resurrection of the church will only come, according to Rusty, when
Christ becomes "the basis for all we say and do." We must walk
away from our marketing and branding, our power-grabbing,

endless consuming, and partisan politics and return to Jesus. The
resurrection of the church is dependent upon our return to a faithful witness of the true gospel of Jesus Christ.

This book follows in the prophetic tradition in the most necessary way. Like Isaiah and Jeremiah, Rusty calls us to let go of
the old world and to welcome the new world God is bringing into
being. Rusty does what any good prophet has done—he names the
problem, and it is not an easy pill for many to swallow. As R.E.M.
said, "It's the end of the world as we know it." The church that
has been co-opted by partisan politics, therapeutic gospels, and
endless consumption must die. We have become something other
than the church we read of in the New Testament. In our pursuit
of numerical growth, we have sold our souls, so to speak, to the
pragmatic ways and means of the world. What we once "used"
to achieve our misguided end is now "using" us, and many have
failed to realize it. But Rusty does not leave us in death. No, that
would go against everything he lives and breathes. While I am very
grateful for his diagnosis of the problem, I am all the more grateful
for his prognosis of resurrection. Part 2 of the book is a must read
for anyone trying to discern the way forward for the church in
the twenty-first century. I am specifically grateful for his discern-
ment that the church of the future in the West will need to look
more like the church did in its first three hundred years. It helps
me to make sense of what I see in the British Isles and especially
in Dundee. Death and resurrection have always been central to
the story of God's people, and this will still be the case for us as we
walk boldly and hopeful into God's future.

God is calling the church to display the new humanity in-
augurated in the resurrection of Jesus Christ. Our worship as
Christians can no longer be defined by our sleek, consumer, per-
sonality-oriented Sunday services, especially when we use worship
as a reference to an experience. To define our worship as "singing
on Sundays" is like defining marriage purely in romantic terms
and avoiding the other more tedious aspects like washing dishes,
doing laundry, listening, serving, being patient, trusting, forgiv-
ing, considering what your spouse needs to flourish, and possibly

caring for children. Without these other things, the marriage is destined for death. In many ways, this is like the commercialized, overly romantic picture of discipleship we have in the church in the West. We have focused so much on marketing personalities, branding worship, and consolidating power that we have made more groupies than disciples of Jesus. I am convinced that Rusty is right to call us to a kind of church that instead looks more like the early church. This is not a call to throw everything out and start all over, but rather to prune, refine, and repent for the ways in which we have participated in the corruption of the church and its message.

Over the last two years in Dundee, our small church plant has turned into forty-five committed adults along with eighteen children. Our numerical growth is only the by-product of our embodied faithfulness to the gospel of Jesus Christ. We do not have any flashy marketing, but we do have a desire that help people know, love, and follow Jesus. We do not have a senior pastor, but we do have a flat leadership that is committed to empowering people based upon their calling and gifting rather than gender, age, or education. We do not have a traditional church building, but we do have many homes to gather in, as well as Blend and the pavilion in the park in the summer. We do not have much money, but we are debt-free. Also, because we are all bi-vocational, we are able to give away more than 70 percent of our church income to those in need. We do not have professional worship experiences, but everyone is welcome to join us as we sit in the round, pray together, sing, discuss the Word in small groups, proclaim the gospel of the kingdom, and gather around the table that is a weekly eucharistic meal rather than a token rite. We try really hard not to make things busy or overly complicated with daily programs and bureaucracy. Rather, we try to keep things simple and to be disciples of Jesus who join in the mission of God in our everyday, ordinary life together. I am not suggesting we get it right all the time or that we do not have any problems. It is just that our issues are very different than the church whose missional apparatus is modelled after big businesses such as McDonald's and Google.

Back to Andrew. You will probably imagine that I am going to finish with his life being utterly transformed. Well, you are right! You are right to expect resurrection. Such is the story of the gospel and the church and, yes, Andrew! Andrew is a completely different person today from the man I met almost two years ago. In fact, I just received a message from Andrew asking if he could take Dayna and I out for dinner on August 14 to celebrate that day we met! But resurrection did not come because the one-and-only Jerry Maguire visited Dundee and preached a therapeutic message with an awesome band that led to a hand being raised in response. Like most of the rest of our culture, Andrew would never have come to such an event. No, it was because there was a small-batch church of former "Jerry Maguires" who moved to Dundee, shared life with Andrew, worked with him, grieved with him when his father later died, surprised him with a birthday party, helped him move houses, studied Scripture with him, and constantly directed him to Jesus in all they did and said. Like Rusty, I long for the day when the world says of today's church what they said of the early church: "Look . . . how they love one another . . . and how they are ready to die for each other."[1] The church must become known for practicing what it preaches. People are leaving, have left and will continue to leave if we do not become what God has made us to be—the church of the crucified and resurrected Jesus.

In 2008/09, Rusty and I lived and ministered together in Perthshire, Scotland. We shared a lot of life together, discipling young adults with Trinity Church in Perth. More than a decade later, I can still remember a particular conversation with Rusty about the state of the church in the West. He compared it to the blockbuster movie *Titanic*. One of the iconic scenes in that film occurs when the extent of the tragedy is finally being realized by the privileged few, and the band is told to keep on playing as though nothing is wrong. Like the *Titanic*, the church is sinking, yet the band is still playing. Many are still trying to deny the problems so clearly laid out in this book because they feel compelled or have been told to protect at all costs the machine which they have

1. Kreider, *Patient Ferment of the Early Church*, 133.

created. The sheer size of what we have created as well as our own pride and ego makes us blind to icebergs. Like the Titanic, whose leadership ignored seven warnings about icebergs, the church has seemingly ignored the warnings that have been sounding us for years.

My prayer is that we, the church, will listen to the prophetic voices like Rusty's, stop the band, call a solemn assembly, confess our corruption, dismantle broken systems, and allow God to resurrect something new, faithful, and fit for the purpose at hand—that heaven and earth might meet in our life together.

Derrick Thames
Dundee, Scotland
August 2020

PART I

The Death of the Church in North America

Chapter 1

INTRODUCTION

THE CHURCH COULD LEARN a lot from Luke Skywalker near the end of his life. I know, I know, many people hate *The Last Jedi*.[1] I would love to explain in more detail why they are all wrong, and why they should love it. Instead, let me simply state that regardless of one's feelings for the movie itself, many of Luke's statements in the film should be received as signposts for the church in North America in the twenty-first century. In particular, we should notice Luke's repeated identification of the all but dead Jedi Order as a "religion." Many react negatively to this description, but if you consider the lore and in particular a lot of what is depicted in the animated series *Clone Wars* and also *Star Wars Rebels*, the description of the Jedi as a religion is apropos. Simply put, a religion is a theory or set of beliefs commonly adhered to, about things such as the origin of all things, the divine, and the purpose of life. Furthermore, such religious beliefs are typically fostered and strengthened by practices peculiar to the religion in question. The Jedi believe that all things are composed of tiny, unobservable bits of matter called midichlorians. Buried deep in their lore is the belief in a strange planet called Mortis, which, under typical circumstances, cannot be navigated to or located. Three godlike creatures dwell there, which appear to be both beyond, and possibly the source of, the force. Jedi believe that the purpose of life is

1. *Star Wars: The Last Jedi.*

3

balance, and specifically balance between the light and dark sides of the force. And finally, Jedi embrace practices such as apprenticeships, meditation, and self-denial in order to achieve balance and oneness with the force. Make no mistake, this is weird stuff indeed, and it all definitely trades upon the religious.

Moreover, Luke clearly believes that the Jedi religion is archaic and all but dead. He describes the sacred original Jedi texts, like himself, as "the last of the Jedi religion." To which he basically says, "Good riddance," many times in *The Last Jedi*. In one important line delivered to Rey, his would-be Padawan or apprentice, Luke states, "Now that they are extinct, the Jedi are romanticized and deified. But if you strip away the myth and look at their deeds, the legacy of the Jedi is failure, hypocrisy, and hubris." He goes on to state the complicit role of the Jedi in the Clone Wars and the rise of the Empire, saying that they failed miserably at their one task: to prevent the rise of the Sith. Instead, the Jedi became the enforcers of the Empire, effectively embracing the role of both chaplain and special forces within a complex version of civil religion (see chapter 3). Luke points out that the Jedi even provided much of the training of the one who would eventually lead the Empire's army: Anakin Skywalker / Darth Vader.[2]

In his frustration with the Jedi order, Luke even goes so far as to half-heartedly attempt to destroy the old tree/temple on the island that houses the original Jedi texts. The weight of the failure of the Jedi, and his own perceived failure in particular, finally got to Luke and he was ready for it all to end. It is at this point that something truly weird and important happens. The great Jedi master Yoda appears and speaks to Luke, despite having died long ago. Always the teacher, Yoda appears to use the force to do that which Luke ultimately could not: destroy the tree/temple. As the tree/temple burns, Yoda says these words to his former Padawan or apprentice: "We must pass on failure—the greatest teacher." Clearly the use of the word *failure* is no mere coincidence. Grizzly old Luke

2. Of course, and as Rey points out, the Jedi—namely Luke Skywalker—do ultimately succeed in defeating Darth Vader and the emperor through the teachings of the Jedi.

feels like a failure. He believes the Jedi have failed. The resistance has failed. He has failed. Yoda neither confirms nor denies this. Instead, he states his opinion that where there is failure, teaching can occur. In speaking of the young force-filled woman Rey, and probably also of Luke himself, Yoda says, "We are what they grow beyond. That is the burden of all masters." It would seem that Luke doesn't need to save the galaxy or train a whole slew of new Jedi. Instead, he is needed to mentor and train just one. In this way, the Jedi—and certainly the force—will never die.

So what does all of this have to do with the church? Like Luke Skywalker, I believe it is time for the church to accept that it is a religion—a weird one at that—that appears to be dying off, and that much of this is the result of our own failures. If a religion is, as I have defined it, a set of beliefs and practices commonly adhered to, about things such as the origin of all things, the divine, and the purpose of life, then Christianity is most certainly a religion. This seems obvious, but the importance of this assertion cannot be overstated in the post-religious Western world. Christians believe that an omnipotent God created the world (out of nothing, mind you), and that this God created the world with purpose. This claim may or may not line up with the scientific teaching of the "big bang," but this alignment surely ends when volition or purpose is ascribed to this creative moment. Christians believe in a God, that there is only one real God, and that this God is Triune: Father, Son, and Spirit. Furthermore, Christians hang the bulk, if not the entirety, of their claims about divinity on the scandalous particularity of the incarnation. According to which the Son was born of a virgin, lived a fully material life amid creation, and then died on the cross as a terrorist threat to the Roman Empire. It should be mentioned, of course, that the belief that this Jesus was resurrected on the third day, and that this resurrection unto new and redeemed life is offered to all who believe and follow Jesus. As a part of this belief, Christians do strange things like baptism and especially the Eucharist, in which they claim to eat the body and drink the blood of Christ until he comes again. This is awfully bizarre and grotesque language even if it is used in a purely memorialist fashion—which many if not most Christian traditions reject. Most believe that in the Eucharist something actually happens, in some capacity, to the elements themselves, or in the mystical experience of receiving the elements. The degree of this "something" differs greatly among the various traditions of the Christian church. Furthermore, Christians believe that God did not need to create, but desired to create in order to have beings to love and be in relationship with. Christians furthermore believe that God did this despite the depths of sin that would emerge, in order that God could redeem and restore creation, eventually existing in a renewed, loving relationship with creation. Finally, Christianity is certainly a religion that is fostered and strengthened by peculiar practices such as the observation of both Sabbath and the Lord's Day, baptism, Eucharist, almsgiving, and general care for the poor, to name only a few. If you add all of this up, we Christians are peculiar at best and downright strange at worst. Indeed, in some cases, we might even be thought to be enemies of the state and of the common good, given our antiquated social views on things we are not supposed to question, such as personal happiness in all of its different roots and forms. Christianity is a religion and as such it is viewed as weird and even threatening in an increasingly post-religious world.

What's wrong with religion anyway? The critique of religion has been around long before Jefferson Bethke's viral video, "Why I Hate Religion, But Love Jesus," but this video has been hugely influential on many contemporary religious and nonreligious folk alike for much of the past decade. With close to thirty-five million views and almost six hundred thousand "likes," it is hard to downplay the significance of this viral video. Bethke's well-intentioned message neatly summarizes the popular, overly individualized brand of Christian faith that has been growing over the last couple of hundred years, and which is especially prevalent today. "Jesus > religion . . . Religion is just behavior modification . . . Religion makes slaves but Jesus makes sons (and surely daughters too), etc." Or, to put it simply, religion = legalistic works righteousness, whereas to follow Jesus is about having faith. This is all very nicely packaged in Bethke's spoken-word production. And again, I have no reason to question his intentions or the power of his testimony of transformation from addiction to drugs, alcohol, and pornography to being a true follower of Jesus. Truth is, the church needs critics like Bethke. The church needs to be constantly reawakened from dogmatic slumber as people like Rich Mullins, Dietrich Bonhoeffer, Karl Barth, John Wesley, Martin Luther, Theresa of Avilla, Julian of Norwich, Francis, Anselm, and Augustine (et al.) have attested to across the church's history. Jesus was, indeed, opposed to "works righteousness," and yet he espoused a curiously active faith. He most certainly employed the term *doulos* or slave/servant to refer to followers of God—saying that everyone will be a *doulos* to something in the end—and we can only serve one thing. Paul certainly picks this theme up and runs with it, yes, but without Paul's bold proclamations of the gospel of the risen christ, we wouldn't have a New Testament today. Faith is not mental assent, or even a "feeling of absolute dependence," as Schleiermacher espoused, but it is a transformative lifestyle. We are better off to think of faith in terms of praxis, as our Latin American friends have suggested.[3] The Christian faith is absolutely "behavior modification," as Bethke critiques in the video, or else he would not boast of being delivered from his various addictions (behaviors) in the name of Christ. His behavior has been modified by the power of the Holy Spirit and, I would presume, those destructive behaviors replaced with acts of service and love. The end result is transformative faith, lived out with others. I believe that is what Bethke hopes for. Unfortunately, he falls victim to the tired old critique of Christianity vis-à-vis religion that has been around for a long time. If I'm correct about the end result, though, I think Bethke is on to something—but not what he thought he was on to. What Bethke is on to is a reformation of the Christian religion in line with the principles of the Reformation which are just as helpful today as they were five hundred years ago: *Reformed semper reformanda* or reformed and always reforming. Our goal should not be to scrap Christianity or reduce it to the notion of a privatized faith, but instead to continually reform its public and private elements so that it is capable of

3. Gutierrez, *Theology of Liberation.*

producing and equipping disciples of Jesus—disciples who are to live out their discipleship with one another, amid and in front of the world, in the hopes that others might see, hear, and desire to know, love, and serve God as well.

Religion is most certainly not a bad thing. It can, though, become stale, oppressive, and even dead/deadly. Christianity is always in danger of becoming #toxicreligion, in today's vernacular. Christianity is constantly in need of freshening up, reformation, and renewal. With the help of the Holy Spirit, this is precisely our calling. As we follow after Jesus we live into the call of discipleship. Our attitudes and actions are modified and changed. We grow and mature in faith. We become part of something much bigger than ourselves: an enormous group of people spanning both space and time, collectively called to live transformed lives of holiness for the sake of the world. The only reason for such transformed lives is an encounter with the living God revealed in Jesus by the Holy Spirit as attested to in both Scripture and tradition. This encounter reframes and shapes one's views on the origin of all things, the divine, and the purpose of life. Such an experience is an overarching meta-experience that brings with it a metanarrative—whether we like this or not. Such an experience is an invitation to join in with countless others in the pursuit of Jesus. This is a religion, and it is something we should not be ashamed of.

That being said, being a part of this religion will surely bring us shame! Religions are weird. They observe weird and different holidays from the world around them—or they make different and competing claims about the nature and purpose of holidays. They are known from the outside by their common practices: what they do and do not do. They affirm a larger story behind all things, a story that defines, shapes, and gives purpose and direction to all things. Religions typically make claims about truth and its particularity that are bizarre, outdated, narrow-minded, and often scandalous. Religions change much more slowly than broader culture, if at all. Religions often claim that truth and meaning can be found by learning from the past, rather than blazing one's own path into the future. Religious folk eat different things, or abstain from things everyone else likes (like bacon and alcohol!). Religious folk dress peculiarly and sometimes even do strange things with their bodies (think tattoos, piercings, and even circumcision). What is more, religious folk tend to think that all aspects of their lives come under the leadership and authority of their religion, and so even "private" matters like sexuality are shaped and determined by their beliefs. In short, religions and religious folk are weird! This is certainly true of religions that we are not a part of! As a Christian, I can say that not only have I heard this, but I have even been guilty of this sort of thinking myself. We often think the other is weird. Jews are weird, Muslims are weird, Hindus are weird, etc. . . . Why not apply the same filter to ourselves and face up to reality: we are a religion and a downright weird one at that! The Christian religion, with its roots in Judaism, filtered through the life teachings of Jesus, as taught by Scripture and tradition, makes claims on every aspect of life. At its best, such claims are not dictated and never forced, but are encouraged and should be voluntarily taken on by those that believe in Jesus and desire to follow him. Not everyone agrees on the specificities of such claims and the practices that result, but all who follow Jesus should agree that following him requires active faith, with and for others. These followers join in with countless others around the world and across time in pursuit of their Messiah, the Christ, Jesus. There can be no other responsible way of understanding such a phenomena than as that of a religion.

Luke is surely not the last Jedi—that's the point of the title, after all. And Star Wars fans know that there are, at least, other Jedis or Padawans that never completed their training out there somewhere in the Star Wars universe. But Luke feels like the last Jedi and certainly it seems that way for much of Episode VIII. He's alone, and not many seem interested in the Jedi's antiquated beliefs anymore. The church in North America finds itself in a position quite similar to that of Luke Skywalker in Episode VIII. It is declining at a speed that is too great to fathom. There are numerous studies that document this. Some have suggested that this will only increase on a very large scale, as the church has basically lost an entire generation or two given its recent political maneuverings and partnerships. Pastoring in places like Seattle and the San Francisco Bay Area has given me a glimpse into the coming reality of secular North American culture. Very few people go to church. And, when megachurches are factored out, what's left are very small gatherings. Where there is growth at all, it is usually to be found in churches that reflect various ethnic and linguistic communities other than white and English-speaking. Increasingly people know nothing about the church, and what they do know, or think they know, is negative. People do not want to go to church and they do not operate from a mindset that gives any precedence to Christian culture. As a former pastor of mine used to ask, "How do you pastor in a setting where people believe they will have to take a moral step down in order to walk into a church?"[4] For most, the church is weird, irrelevant, hateful, bigoted, homophobic, and useless. Statistics easily support this claim and indicate that this trend will only continue.

Finally, if the church is dying off in North America, we have to accept that it is largely our doing. From the beginning the church in North America has played a dangerous game called civil religion, in which it is very difficult to maintain fidelity to the teachings of Jesus over and against those of the state. All too often, to be a Christian was confused with being an American. This mistaken identity has had a terrible price. As Jesus warns, no one can serve two masters. Additionally, the relative comfort afforded to the church allowed it to focus on things such as large and ornate buildings, bloated salaries, large staffs made up of ministry specialists, and evangelistic crusades. Assuming that the church ought to be really large, churches focused a large amount of effort and especially money on evangelism tactics aimed at winning converts, filling pews, and hopefully, gaining tithes. For far too long, emphasis was given to soul-winning rather than disciple-making. As a result, the number of those that identified as Christians

4. This is a claim made often by my former district superintendent on the Washington Pacific District of the Church of the Nazarene, Rev. Jerry Kester, in speaking about the challenges of ministering to a culture that believes itself to be morally superior to the church. This is a challenging position for a church that is used to claiming the moral high ground.

skyrocketed in the United States in particular. The cost of this growth is only now being assessed. In order to grow, many have argued that the church peddled a grossly watered-down version of its message aimed not at transformation but simply at mental assent. The resulting faith that grew out of such evangelistic crusades has been aptly described as *moral therapeutic deism*. This can be understood as generic moral teachings aimed at personal growth and happiness within the framework of a good and benevolent God who wants you to be happy. Unfortunately, the roots of such a message are very shallow, as is the faith it engenders. Too often, when tragedy, loss, financial difficulty, and all manner of philosophical and religious questions arise, believers in this weakened version of Christianity find their faith wanting and move on to allegedly greener pastures such as self-help, CrossFit, and Sunday brunches at wineries.[5]

In the first part of this book, I intend to pointedly diagnose the current state of the church in North America. Using both biblical and agrarian imagery, I will suggest that the soil of North America has been poisoned by poor and overwhelming practices of evangelism and Christian witness. As part and parcel of the poisoning of the soil, I will then explore the issue of civil religion in North America—an original sin, of sorts, for the church in North America. Despite formal claims to the separation of church and state, my position is that the church undercut its potential to flourish by wedding itself, both formally and informally, to the apparatus of the nation-state. Moving forward, I will look at the popular message increasingly proclaimed by the church in North America (and certainly elsewhere), moral therapeutic deism. Not only has the soil been poisoned, the actual seeds being planted are not hearty. Finally, I will examine the pervasive effects of consumerism on the church, and consider the sort of church that results from growing under such conditions. These seeds are not consistent

---

5. It is also worth noting the curious reality that this trend also seems to occur when people's lives are exceedingly comfortable and stable. It becomes easy for people to drift away from faith when it does not seem to benefit them either in their suffering or their comfort.

with the ancient Christian faith. The results are often—but certainly not always—stunted, unfit plants (churches), incapable of proper growth and fruit-bearing. Moreover, in many cases, the seeds have turned out to not even be for the same plant as was originally intended. Finally, I will examine recent trends in church attendance as well as the rise of the "nones" and "uns," or those of no faith or even an anti-faith. What happens when so many leave the church and when so many are opposed to the church? This is the future that we are heading toward and which we are already experiencing as the church in North America. In many ways, I believe the current model or form of the church in North America is dying. Perhaps this is a good thing? For lest this book be a tragedy, I would point out the core of the gospel: resurrection. Ours is a God of resurrection, and resurrection comes only after and through death. In the book of Revelation, God self-identifies as the "God who makes all things new." My contention is that much of the newness comes through, and in spite of, death. So perhaps the church, like you and I—all of us—will die. So too, though, will the church be raised to new life in Christ. It is to this task I will turn in the second section of this book.

In part 2 I will embrace the seeming death of the church as the very means by which God will resurrect the church. First, I will propose that the future of the church in North America will look much more like the first few centuries of the church's existence than the last seventeen or so. In other words, the future of the church in North America is as a missionary movement of small, authentic communities stripped of much of the structure that has come to define the contemporary church: large buildings, large paid staffs, and elaborate programed ministries. The future of the church in North America is small, communal, countercultural, and, I think, much more authentic. Next, I will examine what it will mean for the church to exist in relationship to the nation-state or empire apart from civil religion. Here, I will suggest a return to the politics of Jesus as Christian witness both for and against the state. The next section continues the trend of setting forth a resurrected view of the things that caused the church to fail in North

America. Here we will examine the gospel itself and attempt to recover the simple, New Testament, and Pentecost message that first caused the church to flourish. I will suggest a return to this simple life- and world-changing message. Finally, I will conclude with a prescriptive chapter asking the question, "What are we left with?" What sort of church will this resurrected church be? At this stage, it will be important to consider the role of the church in North America in relation to the global church—especially the church in the global South. How might we learn from our sisters and brothers in places like Central and South America, India, and Africa? My hope is that we can also be a blessing to them, as they will eventually have to deal with the same market-driven secularization that those of us in the North and especially West have brought upon ourselves. Together, we are the church, and together, our future will be bright.

In the end, then, this book is not a bleak tragedy, but instead a bright comedy. What first appears to be death is only the opportunity for resurrection. God has constituted the church, and God will not allow it to fail. That said, we must accept that much of what we know of as the church today is nonessential and perhaps even inherently damaging. As much of the structure of the contemporary church dies, the church will be offered the opportunity for new life—a life that will look much more like our origins in the first three centuries than the time of our alleged flourishing on the backs of empire and colonization. The church will not die once and for all. But the church will go through death into resurrection. May God deal graciously with us as we adjust to this difficult and yet promising future.

Chapter 2

POISONED SOIL

A Diagnosis of the Current State of the Church in North America

AMERICA, AS IT TURNS out, is no place for old deities. Or so Neil Gaiman would have us believe in his fictitious work *American Gods*.[1] (Spoiler alert!) No stranger to ancient religious works, especially of the folk and mythical nature, Gaiman weaves together religions and their deities in a fascinating, novel, and I would argue appropriately terrifying manner. In short, Gaiman's story rests on the notion that North America, and the United States in particular, is where deities come to die. Gaiman suggests that deities live, move, and have their being predicated upon the lips, prayers, beliefs, and practices of their supplicants. As various people groups migrated across the globe, therefore, whether by choice or force, so too did their gods. American soil, though, it would turn out, would prove to be effectively lethal for these various and sundry deities. This secular soil would, in turn, give rise to the gods of secular modernity, the no-gods that sit in the seat of God(s), to borrow a key concept from Barth's second commentary on Paul's Letter to the Romans. These gods include, but are not limited to, TV, mobile phones, the internet, electricity, social media, marketing, and progress. As belief and adoration of the older Gods

1. Gaiman, *Annotated American Gods.*

14

such as YHWH, Odin, Ba'al, Shiva, and the many lesser deities and spirits waned in North America, belief and worship of the newer forms of deity rose, and indeed continue to rise. Gaiman deftly points out that these technologies and philosophies depend equally on passionate belief and unwavering adoration from their supplicants, as did the older religions. The trick is that these are presented to us as nonreligious, amoral, and depoliticized; neutral entities to be used, and not as things that use us. And so, as people grow more and more skeptical of "religion" and incredulous toward all blatant metanarratives, newer, subtler belief systems and meta-narratives have taken our minds and, indeed, bodies captive. This eliminates the life-support system for the various older deities and spirits resulting in their death or, at best, a comatose-like state of hibernation. No real diagnosis is offered for how or why this happened. Instead, the mysteriously hard, dry, infertile religious soil of North America seems simply hopeless for gods and their subsequent religions. As the book ends, it seems that whatever life remains for the few of the old gods who remain in North America will be the life of one living in a wasteland, stripped bare of all that is valuable for nutrition and survival. These gods will need to resort to trickery, moreso than ever before, and even then, they will barely cling to existence. Of course, Gaiman's work is fictitious. But like all great works of fiction, it has real-world starting points, resonances, and implications. Is there a sense in which *American Gods* might serve as a prophetic work of cultural exegesis of the secularized world in which we live?[2] Just what is the state of the contemporary Christian church in North America?[3]

2. Having used the term *secular* several times now, I would be remiss not to refer readers to Charles Taylor's incredibly poignant work, *A Secular Age*. Every pastor, indeed every thinking person in the "West," ought to read this book. Andrew Root has recently published two important works engaging Taylor's work from a pastoral perspective: *Faith Formation in a Secular Age* and *The Pastor in a Secular Age*. I highly recommend these works as well.

3. For the purposes of this book, the Christian faith will be exclusively examined. Admittedly, though, such examinations are surely also worthwhile for other religions or belief systems. Furthermore, by "Christian church" or "the church" I am attempting to be inclusive of the various branches of the Christian faith, including Eastern Orthodoxy, Roman Catholicism, and Protestantism

The Pew Research Center's 2014 Religious Landscape Study revealed staggering statistics regarding the changing role of the church in North America.[4] Some 70.6 percent of those polled identified as Christian, with roughly two-thirds of these identifying as Protestants and one-third as Roman Catholics. This number was down almost 8 percent from the previous study conducted seven years prior. At the same time, nearly 6 percent identify as holding to a non-Christian religious viewpoint, which was up 1.2 percent from the previous study. Perhaps most telling of all, the percentage of those who identity as holding to no form of religious belief system rose from 16 percent in 2007 to almost 23 percent in 2014. This means that almost one in four people, as of 2014, identify as non-Christian, often called a "none" or a person of no faith. Meanwhile, a 2018 Gallup poll places the numbers at a much starker level, claiming that only about 50 percent of Americans identify as belonging to one of the three historic monotheistic religions: Christianity, Judaism, or Islam.[5] This number is further broken down according to various qualifiers such as age, gender, ethnicity, and race in such a way as to indicate an extremely difficult course ahead for the church (as well as the synagogue and mosque) in North America. Additionally, related research from the Pew Research Center reveals that in 2013 only about 37 percent of Americans actually attend church services weekly.[6] This means that of the 70 percent of people that claim to be Christians, less than half attend church services regularly. As a longtime pastor, I think it's fair to point out that both research and personal experience would challenge the truthfulness of this number—and remember this number is over five years old! Thus, it is safe to say that in reality, only about 25 percent or one in four of Americans regularly attend a church. Honestly, that still seems like a bloated number to me! In

---

and all of its branches. This work will pertain most directly to the Protestant and evangelical branches of the Christian faith, though it is, I believe, pertinent to all who would call themselves Christian.

4. Pew, "America's Changing Religious Landscape."

5. Gallup, "Church Membership Down Sharply."

6. Pew, "What Surveys Say about Worship Attendance."

fact, it's my understanding that the average churchgoing Christian attends church just around two times a month. My experiences confirm this.

Remember, these numbers reflect the United States as a whole.[7] What would happen if we look to one of the more extremely secularized places in the continent such as the San Francisco Bay Area or Seattle? These areas are important to me because I've spent the last six years pastoring in these two places, first in Seattle, and then in the East San Francisco Bay Area. The 2014 Pew Study revealed that only 48 percent of people living the San Francisco metro area identified as a Christian, with 15 percent identifying as people of non-Christian faiths, and over 35 percent as nones or people of no faith. Only 22 percent stated that they attended a worship service weekly. If we add five years on to this study, and trend in the same direction the research was going, that means that between 10 to 20 percent of people in the San Francisco Metropolitan area claim to attend church regularly, which means one, maybe two out of every ten people. At a recent conference I attended it was reported that as few as 3 percent of people actually attend a Christian church weeky in this area. Research suggests that much of the rest of the United States is moving in this same direction, though not quite as steeply. This is the sort of parched, worn out soil I'm thinking of. This is why Gaiman's fictitious account comes to mind when I think about the church in North America. How did this happen?

Before we address the how, let us first consider two major misconceptions that many of my well-meaning colleagues like to fall back on as cure-all antidotes for this depressing diagnosis. Silver bullets, if you will, able to thwart the big bad wolf in one quick motion. The first of these so-called silver bullets comes in the form of the various teachings Jesus gives about the field being ripe for harvest if there are just enough workers.

---

7. North America is often cited, but the research being done is typically only reflective of the United States. If we were to include all of North America, Canada would reveal even lower numbers of churchgoers, while Mexico would likely reveal a higher percentage of those that identify as Christians.

1. "But I tell you, look around you, and see how the fields are ripe (*leukai*) for harvesting."[8]

2. "Then he said to his disciples, 'The harvest is plentiful (*polus*), but the laborers are few.'"[9]

3. "He said to them, 'The harvest is plentiful (*polus*), but the laborers are few; therefore ask the Lord of the harvest to send out laborers into his harvest.'"[10]

Too often, these statements made by Jesus are employed as proof-texts, or unconditional promises for us to hold on to, that if we will simply go into the harvest fields (or preach and serve), then we will harvest (or save souls) and thus attendance will grow. The last bit is crucial. We can dance around this all we want but at the end of the day, every strategy-driven, tactic-oriented lesson I've ever seen or received assumes that if things are done "right" growth, and yes, numerical growth, will happen. "'The field is ripe for the harvest,' right?" "If you will go, or if more will respond to the call to preach the gospel, *your church* will grow." You've attended the same conferences, workshops, and trainings I've attended, haven't you?! What if these are not proof-texted statements to "name and claim" but rather general truth statements given to Jesus' closest followers, who were called to share the gospel and their very lives with an un-evangelized world? These were metaphorical images, after all, given to the disciples to help them understand their calling and to lovingly urge them into action. These statements have specific temporal and geographical context and are not general future-oriented statements.

What if at some point we can no longer expect such large harvests? What if we began using unsustainable, or even unhealthy tactics to try to boost our harvest? What if we used spiritual GMOs, if you will, or simply over-farmed the land, and now our methods are catching up with us?

8. John 4:35b New Revised Standard Version. All future biblical references will be to the NRSV.

9. Matt 9:37.

10. Luke 10:2.

This leads me to the second misconception or silver bullet, found in Jesus' declaration that he will build his church on Peter and that "the gates of Hades will not prevail against it."[11] Does this mean that the church will continue to grow as it did during Christendom? Or, does it simply mean that it will not ever be destroyed or defeated? Does this statement ensure unending growth until the eschaton, or is it a statement of security and provision amid the threat of persecution and ultimately destruction? Surely it is the latter and not the former. Here again, this statement is not a guarantee of advancement or growth, but an ultimate promise that the powers of evil will never overcome the church—as they would never truly overcome Jesus. And, we must remember, this was certainly put to the test in the crucifixion of Jesus. Jesus did appear to lose the battle with evil—at least for awhile. Whatever loss was sustained, though, was only fleeting and not permanent. Likewise, I believe that Jesus was making a promise in kind to Peter, and subsequently to all who would gather in the name of Jesus by the power of the Holy Spirit. This simple and yet powerful statement therefore, did not guarantee constant, unending growth, but rather ensured protection against ultimate destruction. The church's fate, in other words, was to be intimately wrapped up in the fate of her bridegroom, Jesus.

It is here that I need to point out that this book is not a work of doom and gloom. This is not a work of death, but rather a work about resurrection—death and resurrection is how I will try to write about this subject. We must remember that resurrection necessarily involves death. We shouldn't speak of resurrection without speaking of death. There is no way around this uncomfortable truth. This book, like the world in which we live, is going to get bleaker before it gets brighter. And even then, the end result may not be what you are looking for. My apologies ahead of time, if this is the case. My hope, though, is that Jesus will be found and remembered in the end. Along the way I hope that we will be strengthened in the resolve that despite entering into a time very unlike the last few hundred years, the church will survive, and

11. Matt 16:18.

even thrive, but according to very different metrics than those we currently are willing to use. My contention, and this will be made quite clear in the second half of the book, is that there will indeed always be a harvest, and that the gates of hell will not prevail against the church. That said, I don't think it is reasonable to expect continued results like were experienced during Christendom—nor do I think that the so-called results were always kingdom results. But we will get to that later.

To be clear, then, the church will continue to grow. New converts will be received. Transformation will take place. New life will spread. The goodness of God is unrelenting, after all. This is not being challenged. The point of contention is whether or not this will occur at the pace it has previously, and what will happen to the large institutional church in North America. The fact remains, that while the harvest continues (indeed it will never stop), people are leaving the church in droves. Brunches, CrossFit, kid's sports, and Costco runs have supplanted church attendance. This is not necessarily new, but the rate of it is. What is new is that open adherence to atheism, nihilism, generic spirituality, or even anti-Christianity has supplanted basic Christian faith. In some cases, alternative forms of faith such as Islam, or various "Eastern" religions have gained converts from the ranks of former Christians. But by and large, people are leaving with a mind to not replace faith or the church at all.

My own experience has confirmed this reality. I often joke about it, but in truth my experience is that telling someone I am a pastor can be likened to telling them that I have the plague. A recent Gallup poll confirms that clergy are now in the middle of the playing field in terms of trusted professions, with a startling number of "low/very low" rankings.[12] With the almost constant flow of child abuse and inappropriate conduct stories plaguing the clergy these days I'm not sure I would challenge these numbers. The average person no longer trusts the clergy or holds us in high regard. We are seen as managers of a hypocritical, homophobic, racist, oppressive, and certainly antiquated religion that has

12. McCarthy, "America's Most & Least Trusted Professions."

nothing to offer enlightened and liberated minds. We have failed to deliver on our promises of peace and the love of Christ, instead offering up judgmental, hypocritical, and divisive systems that don't seem to serve personal needs any longer. And so, people are leaving, and they will continue to leave. What is the church to do?

An attempt at answering this most important question will come in the second half of this book. At present, let me simply suggest what the church must not do is remain ignorant to the realities highlighted above. Neither should the church pretend that things are better than they are. We must face reality. Much, if not most of the Western world simply has no time, interest, or trust left to give to the church. New gimmicks, strategies, or hip clothing won't change this. Preaching louder, longer, or more boldly won't change this. Blurring the lines between the church and the world, setting aside doctrine, and all things "religious," won't work either. None of these things will "work." This is to say if "work" is understood by the old metrics that served us so well for the last couple hundred years (and indeed millennia). We must give up our obsession with growing large, significant, powerful, or anything else grandiose and instead we must simply desire to be faithful, accepting along the way that our numbers will be fewer, our power and influence will wane, and the features that we've taken for granted as normative for church structure and polity for so long will go away. Yes, I believe all of this will happen, or indeed is already happening, and yes, I believe this is a good thing. I also think there's not much we can do about it. So why not settle in and rediscover our faith during this time of change, death, and resurrection?

At a recent gathering of church leaders I was given a pack of heirloom tomato seeds. The seeds were an illustration in support of a sermon delivered by a very well-meaning denominational leader about the need for growth in an ever-changing world. Let me make it clear that I loved the sentiment. Heirloom tomatoes rather than homogenized, GMO-ified seeds. The image of small-plot or raised-bed urban gardening. Not only are these trendy images, but they are fitting for the climate we live in, especially for those of us living in the Bay Area. The only problem was that behind the talk of different tactics and harder-to-grow plants was the same assumption: if you plant it, it will grow. Repeatedly we were admonished that the seed possessed all that was necessary to grow. But this is not right, is it? What happens when you scatter seeds on concrete? Nothing. To stick with the New Testament imagery of farming as evangelism we must remember that we are told that certain soil allows for growth while other sorts of soil do not allow for growth.[13] Jesus teaches that in addition to good soil, rain, and sunshine are needed—and these are basically out of our control.[14] And finally, we're also reminded, pointedly by Paul, that we often never reap or even see the results of our planting.[15] Moreover, sometimes "the enemy" corrupts our work by planting weeds throughout the good seeds.[16] The result is that the weeds will choke out many of the good plants, but some of the good plants will still grow—they will not be thwarted. And to add one more challenge, what if we, ourselves, have poisoned the soil or over-farmed to the point that the land is simply infertile? What then can we expect but a small, stunted crop?

The result is something like this. The seed carries all the potential for new plants within itself, but it can't do anything at all unless planted in decent soil, with the right amount of sun and water, and preferably without the presence of enemies or predators who seek to thwart the growing plants. When all these conditions are met, a tomato plant should grow. And as part of its growth, it will bring forth seeds that contain within themselves the potential for new life or new plants. Optimal conditions are always assumed in such a scenario, with the result of fruit and reproductive faith with just a bit of effort and grace. But what happens when the soil that the seeds are planted in to is dry and barren? What if the soil has been so overworked that it is almost completely stripped of the nutrients necessary to allow for and sustain life? What if, moreover, the soil has actually been poisoned by years of bad farming

13. Matt 13:1–23; Mark 4:1–20; Luke 8:1–15.

14. Matt 5:45.

15. John 4:37; 1 Cor 3:6–9.

16. Matt 13:24–30.

practices, aimed at quick, cheap, and somewhat bland fruit?[17] And finally, what if we add to this a world full of enemies, eager to stifle or stunt any possible growth? In this scenario, is it fitting to expect growth from the seeds? And if so, how much growth should we expect? I think the answer is clear: not much. Very little growth should be expected in such circumstances except where a farmer is willing to cultivate good soil, free of sand and rocks, free of the lingering poisons of so many years of bad farming practices. The farmer must seek to shelter her plant from the work of the enemy and world around her, while nonetheless ensuring that the plant is hearty enough to withstand wind and extreme temperatures. Such a plant will surely grow—for indeed the seed possesses all it needs to potentially produce a new plant. Such a plant needs help, though, especially when growing conditions are less than optimal. This, I would suggest, is the future of the church in North America: small, slow, heavily cultivated growth that will not live up to previous expectations for productivity, but which will produce healthy, faithful, fruit capable of reproducing healthy, faithful, and authentic Christian faith.

In the end, I don't think it's fair to interpret Gaiman's ficticious narrative as suggesting that the indigenous soil of North America is inherently inhospitable toward gods and deities. No, Gaimaon's novel thesis seems to assume that Europeans brought these unfavorable conditions with them when they embarked upon the experiment that is America. They sought a world that was as free from superstition and religion as it was from monarchy and morality. They wanted a land where anything goes, so long as one was able to build and defend it. They wanted a land of individualism, manifest destiny, consumerism, and nihilism—even if they didn't know it yet. The result poisoned more than the soil, it poisoned and corrupted the very fabric of human being. If indeed

17. Examples of this include considering the saying of a prayer as conversion without any requirement of discipleship, performing baptisms and even re-baptisms without catechesis, and most forms of televangelism or other sorts of disembodied worship.

humans are *homo religiouso*, as James K. A. Smith has suggested,[18] then North America is producing twisted, perverted versions of what humanity was intended to be.[19] As we move ahead I would like to examine three particularly large sources of the poison that has been introduced to the soil in North America: civil religion, moral therapeutic deism, and consumerism. The effects of these poisons are many, complex, and unrelenting. With toxins such as this present in such large capacities in our soil, it is no wonder that the seeds of faith are beginning to be choked out.

18. Smith, *Desiring the Kingdom*.

19. Athanasius noticed something surprisingly similar in regard to the general effects of sin. Athanasius, *On the Incarnation*.

Chapter 3

GETTING TO THE ROOT
OF THE PROBLEM

Civil Religion

"A Nation is the same people living in the same place."[1]

THE NEXT THREE CHAPTERS will focus on elements that seriously complicate and, in fact, compromise the mission and message of the church in North America. To continue with organic imagery, we will begin with the difficult and rocky soil in which Christianity has had to grow since first European coming to the continent in the fifteenth century. Chapter 4 will focus on the actual seeds that have been and continue to be sown—the seeds of moral therapeutic deism. Then in chapter 5 we will consider consumerism as a form of contamination that constantly seeps in from the surrounding culture, corrupting the plants that do grow—intentionally or not.

> That same day Jesus went out of the house and sat beside the sea. Such great crowds gathered around him that he got into a boat and sat there, while the whole crowd stood on the beach. And he told them many things in parables, saying "Listen! A sower went out to sow. And as he sowed, some seeds fell on the path, and the birds came and ate them up. Other seeds fell on rocky ground,

1. Joyce, *Ulysses*, 317.

where they did not have much soil, and they sprang up quickly; since they had no depth of soil. But when the sun rose, they were scorched; and since they had no root, they withered away. Other seeds feel among thorns, and the thorns grew up and choked them. Other seeds feel on good soil and brought forth grain, some a hundredfold, some sixty, some thirty. Let anyone who has ears listen!" (Matt 13:1–9)

No one can serve two masters; for a slave will either hate the one and love the other, or be devoted to the one and despise the other. You cannot serve both God and wealth/mammon. (Matt 6:24)

The parable of the Sower is very important for the argument of this book. Notice that the seeds that fell on rocky soil took root and grew quickly, only to shrivel and die when the sun rose over the small plants and blasted down its heat and light. Probably a few plants survived, but not many. Their quick growth was negated by their unnatural conditions. What was the primary issue plaguing these small plants? They had little to no root system. The rocky soil would not allow for the seeds to send down roots deep and wide enough to drink up groundwater, preserve nutrients, and even anchor the plants for times of harsh weather. As a result the plants were unable to handle even something that was necessary for their growth, such as the sun.

My take on the growth of the church in North America is much like this parable. While there are definitely seeds that have managed to take root, and are holding strong, I'm afraid that much of what we have are small plants that grew too quickly, in poor and rocky soil, and which do not have much chance of survival. Ironically, one of the primary sources of the rocks in the soil can be traced back to the very people that first brought Christianity to North America. For the purposes of this chapter I would like to identify these so-called rocks as civil religion, or the blending together of civic and religious teachings, values, and practices for the sake of one and usually to the detriment of the other. While in the course of worldwide history the church has certainly taken the dominant role in this relationship at times (think Charlemagne!), I would argue that typically this relationship is one in which the state takes the driver's seat, either brokering a deal with a particular religion, or else simply co-opting it for the sake of control. As Karl Marx accurately described, "religion" in this way certainly can be "the opiate of the masses."[2] Similarly, William Cavanaugh has argued persuasively that whereas the church is often blamed for the corruption that often ensues from civil religion, history reveals that it is actually the state's use of the church—willing or not— that often results in violence and oppression.[3] Civil religion often produces a hybrid political entity, masked in the clothing of the church, but with the power and ambition of statecraft and empire-building—things that should be antithetical to the mission and message of the church. This is exactly what happened in the "new world" from the first day Europeans arrived with the intention of "settling" it.

It is often said that the pilgrims came to the "new land" of North America looking for a place to establish freedom of religion or freedom of worship. In fact, though, these early settlers were looking for a place where their own, hyper-Calvinistic theology and worship might be allowed, free of persecution, to the exclusion of other forms of worship such as Arminianism and Roman Catholicism. Thus the seminal freedom of religion established by the Puritans was a freedom they did not extend to all. Regardless, religion—Christianity in particular—played an integral role in the conquering, settling, and development of the settlements that would eventually become known as the United States of America. The vast majority of the early "settlers" identified as Christian, specifically of the Protestant and Reformed persuasion.[4] They understood their expansion as God-ordained, and desired to establish the official right to worship as they saw fit—something disallowed, or at the very least unwelcomed, in places they came from, such as

2. Marx, *Contribution to the Critique of Hegel's Philosophy of Right.*

3. Cavanaugh, *Myth of Religious Violence.*

4. Of course, the same cannot be said for those who were forced into coming to North America via the trans-Atlantic slave trade.

England or Holland. As a result, the fledgling government of the colonies and then the early republic used intentionally Christian language in its speech and writings. It is the nature and extent of this Christian language used by many of the founding fathers that is the source of the rocks in the soil, to continue with the metaphor. While the United States affirmed the separation of church and state in its seminal documents, many would argue that this affirmation is one of word and not of deed. In fact, it is quite common for people to refer to the United States as a "Christian Nation"—something that seemingly flies in the face of the separation of the church and state.

The notion of any nation being a "Christian Nation" is hard to defend from the basis of Scripture. True, God calls the nation (read people-group and not state or country) of Israel to be God's chosen people, but such status does not seem transferable to others, or repeatable. Jesus is understood, by most, to be the fulfilment and opening up of the covenant made with Israel so that God's covenantal people would no longer be limited to Israelites but would include Gentiles from all tribes and nations. The new reality of the church is offered, in Acts and beyond, as the corporate gathering of people, by God, *out of the nations*, and into the household of God. Many others have addressed this issue, and the difficulty with referring to the United States as a "Christian Nation."[5] I would suggest that it is wise to heed such critiques and thus to be wary of any description of the United States as a "Christian Nation." In fact, I have argued elsewhere that most of the early founding fathers were not so much Christian, as they were Deists in general and Epicureans in particular, seeking to establish a new and greater Athens in North America.[6] To this end, they intentionally co-opted Christian language to gain trust and support, only to twist this support to their purposes. Careful examination of the words used by founders such as Thomas Jefferson, Benjamin Franklin, Thomas Paine, and John Adams reveal a deep penchant for Epicurean and

5. These thinkers include Stanley Hauerwas, John Howard Yoder, Oliver O'Dononvan, and Gregory Boyd.

6. Brian, "Beyond Syncretism."

atomistic philosophy, the likes of which can be found in the Enlightenment work of Galileo, Descartes, Hobbes, Spinoza, Leibniz, Locke, and Giordanno Bruno. Such thinking affirmed a generic God, akin to a "clockmaker" or "architect," but certainly not the Triune God of Christianity as revealed in the person of Jesus of Nazareth.[7] Matthew Stewart has suggested quite persuasively that Thomas Young and Ethan Allen were the primary conduits for this ancient philosophical system and its prevalence in the speech and writings of the founders.[8] An important point made by Stewart, which I highlight in my "Beyond Syncretism," is that the religious and philosophical language of so many of the founders—language that many appeal to today as the basis of the claim that the United States is a "Christian nation"—is in fact an intentional co-opting of Christianity for political purposes. In other words, many of the most important founding fathers intentionally used language that seemed like Christianese, but really was not. The Gods affirmed by the leaders and the followers were two decidedly different Gods. One was the God of Nature, the other the Triune God of Christianity revealed in the scandalous particularity of Jesus of Nazareth. This was done to gain political support and to instill cultic and religious significance for the new nation. The process of co-opting Christianity for the purposes of nationalism and empire-building was careful and subtle. It was very effective. Today, this is seen in the so-called "Religious Right" and the conflation of the church and the United States, especially the Republican Party, by so many Christians, not least of the evangelical persuasion. Historical framework aside, the real issue as it pertains to this project is what civil religion in the United States looks like today, and how it affects the message and future of the church.

7. In short, Epicurus's atomism claims that all matter, everything that exists, must have verifiable natural origins. Matter comes from naturally observable origins and stays in the realm of nature, even upon death. Thus it is impossible to claim that a being, *vis-à-vis* God, who exists outside of time and the created order, could be the foundation for creating anything. Epicurus's thought leads toward either atheistic naturalism or pantheism; and in fact the two might easily be argued to be one and the same.

8. Stewart, *Nature's God*.

Recent events illustrate well the lingering presence of civil religion and why this is to be considered rocky soil for the gospel to grow in. The lack of distance between Christianity and one's political party is quite alarming and should be seen as a primary example of the lingering power and problem of civil religion. The examples given will highlight the confusion between the church and the Republican Party in particular, as these examples are too rampant to not be addressed. It is important to note, though, that the so-called "Christian Left" often appears to be just as blind to the difference between the Christian faith and the Democratic Party.[9] What follows, then, should not be mistaken as an apology for the often incomprehensible views and talking points of the "Christian Left." Instead, the critical commentary on right wing Christian Americans should be understood as coming from an agenda of wanting Christians to relearn the ability to discern between political allegiance, party politics, statecraft, and empire building on the one hand, and the incredibly countercultural way of the gospel on the other. The same should be assumed for the "Christian Left." To be concerned about the gospel, after all, is to be filled with an imaginative vision for the already/not-yet kingdom of God, in such a way that no human political agenda will suffice. Perhaps, then, we must, all of us, be converted to Jesus and to his kingdom.

I will always remember waking up to a strange new United States on Friday morning, November 9, 2016. Though living in Seattle at the time, I awoke in Dayton, Ohio, where I had just undergone PRK (Lasik) eye surgery the day before. I went to bed late the night before with the assumption that Donald Trump would be elected as the president of the United States, dazed with the lingering pain from the surgery and a little off in general because of the pain medication. Still, waking up to the news of the strange outcome of the election, in which Trump lost the popular vote and yet somehow won the election seemed bafflingly un-American. How

9. I worry that the reactionary spirit that characterizes so much of the "Christian Left" might not end up being just as destructive as that which they are critiquing. In fact, it could be argued that both the Christian "right" and "left" are really just two sides of the same coin in that they both seem to assume that American politics is the way to go about seeking change in the world.

can someone lose by millions of votes and yet win? As a pastor and theologian who is deeply concerned with the political nature of the gospel, I knew what this meant: my people, indeed all US citizens, were incredibly divided. No one seemed to really like either candidate. As Dave Chappell quipped, most seemed ashamed to be in line to vote in the first place as neither candidate offered a truly compelling option.[10] I knew that the world in which I had woken up was a different one from the one in which I had fallen asleep.

One of the most important aspects of Trump's election was that he rode the wave of Protestant evangelicalism, as well as white Roman Catholicism, into office. The overwhelming voter base for Donald Trump was made up of those who claim to frequently attend Christian worship services. On the opposite side, those who attended Christian worship services less frequently, or who claim to be "none," voted more for Hillary Clinton. The sad reality is that Trump's voting base was basically the same as all previous Republican candidates, if not slightly higher.

> While earlier in the campaign some pundits and others questioned whether the thrice-married Trump would earn the bulk of white evangelical support, fully eight-in-ten self-identified white, born-again/evangelical Christians say they voted for Trump, while just 16% voted for Clinton. Trump's 65-percentage-point margin of victory among voters in this group—which includes self-described Protestants, as well as Catholics, Mormons and others—matched or exceeded the victory margins of George W. Bush in 2004, John McCain in 2008 and Mitt Romney in 2012.[11]

The easily supported point here is that evangelical Christians and conservative white Roman Catholics vote almost exclusively Republican *regardless of who the party's candidate is!* In the case of Trump, as Jessica Martinez teases, people wondered if perhaps this trend might change. Would his three marriages, corrupt and failed businesses, or refusal to publish tax returns tarnish his image to the

10. Chappelle, *Equanimity* (Netflix, 2017).

11. Martínez, "How the Faithful Voted."

point that the usual Christian Republican voting base would turn aside? Or, perhaps his audacious bullying of reporters, and other candidates, or the recordings of him openly slandering women, even to the point of joking that it was perfectly fine to grab a woman by her genitals—perhaps these moral vices might estrange him from the usual Christian voters. Or finally, perhaps the fact that Trump had no real track record of Christianity himself, and that he had previously taken a pro-choice stance on abortion, would render him ultimately unacceptable. The list goes on. But would any of these factors deter the usual voters? As it turns out, the answer was "no!" In fact, a higher number of self-identifying evangelical Christian voters voted for Trump than the previous Republican presidential candidates. Rather than shy away, evangelical leaders were quick to jump on the Trump bandwagon, especially after he promised to give "power" to the church. One comically tragic picture captures the paradox of the Trump election better than any words I could use. In it, Jerry Falwell Jr. and wife Becki pose with then-candidate Trump in front of a wall of Trump's own magazine covers, including especially the 1990 *Playboy* issue, which featured him on the cover with a scantily clad woman.[12] The point to this is simply that Trump's demonstrable character, or lack thereof, didn't seem to matter to self-identifying evangelical Christians in particular, of whom roughly eight out of ten voted for Trump. Trump said the right things on issues such as abortion, and he promised to restore power to the church in exchange for the vote, and that was enough. Trump's election is clearly an example of the rocky soil of civil religion, according to which the state and the church are intermingled in a confusing manner. Perhaps more importantly, though, his election demonstrates the end result of attempting to grow healthy plants in such rocky soil: eventually most of the plants are choked out and die.

Following the election, a mass exodus began as young people in particular began leaving evangelical traditions in favor of other Christians traditions, though in many cases they left with the intention of claiming no faith or "unfaith" or an anti-(Christian)

12. See "Falwell Dismisses Photo."

faith position. A repeated sentiment I heard from young people all over the nation and on every social media platform was, "How could my parents and grandparents, who taught me the sanctity of marriage as well as the related virtues of chastity and respect for women in particular, and who taught me how to treat those less fortunate than myself, how to be a good sport, etc. . . . how could these same people vote for someone so opposite to all of those values they instilled in me? And, what's more, how could they go one step further in anointing him as God's chosen leader— God's man—for such a time as this?" Young person after young person found themselves thrown up against the unmasked harsh and hypocritical civil religion of their parents and grandparents and they said, "Enough." The church in North America, which was already reeling in many ways, has not been the same since. I fear it never will be.

As clergy, what do we do in response to such situations? As I sat in my hotel room and recalled overly excited and overly scared parishioners on both ends of the spectrum, I realized that my people were deeply divided like the entire nation was divided. I pastored a fairly progressive church in a fairly conservative evangelical Protestant denomination. My people were on the front lines. I had to do something. Knowing that I would miss the service in a few days due to the recovery process from my eye surgery, I crafted an all-church email reminding them of their common bond in Christ, and their ultimate allegiance to him. I asked them to prayerfully consider their brothers and sisters, and to remember that we now had to do the hard work of being one with each other despite differences. I called them to spend time going around giving hugs and handshakes on Sunday morning, passing the peace of Christ, remembering that the peace of Christ was in and with them, and that this peace was far deeper and more unitive than any election, candidate, or government. I tried to be as *via media* or middle of the road as possible, in other words. I tried to console and caution. Ultimately, I tried to call them together to be, as they were always intended to be, the body of Christ in that little corner of the world. I think that my response was a good one, though I'm open to critiques. You will understand my confusion, then, when I was greeted with heavy critique by one of my most faithful and loyal congregants, who also happens to be a strongly right wing, conservative Republican. He was very critical of my letter, accusing me of creating division when there was none there. He "reminded" me that my job was not to be "political" and to leave that stuff outside the church. When I informed him that unbeknownst to him there were many in the congregation that felt differently, he was skeptical. Apparently calling for unity in the midst of clear division and confusion was a problem in that I did not see the election as a giant triumph for Christianity. My friend (who really is a wonderful man) was, like so many others, blinded to the nuances of his own deep-seeded civil religion. He couldn't see that we are always called to more than any political party, candidate, or country can offer—that we are called to be servants of the King and subjects in the kingdom of God.

The problems around the reception of President Trump only continued since his election, and it is safe to say that the United States and the church in the United States are as divided as ever. For the church, in particular, attendance continues to decline, and those who leave are increasingly likely to never return. Many are leaving with the explicit purpose of walking away from their Christian faith, or even embracing a strong position in critique of their former faith. This is quite different from generations past which also saw people leave, but with a laziness or agnostic apathy that would often see them come back around later in life.

Another similar example can be seen in the Alabama state senatorial campaign of Roy Moore. Moore, who had been accused of multiple acts of the sexual abuse of a child, received the overwhelming support of evangelical Christians in the state of Alabama because of his status as a Republican, his verbal claims to Christianity, and his support by President Donald Trump.[13] Moore's campaign was ultimately unsuccessful, but just barely, as he received the overwhelming majority of white and evangelical votes in Alabama. The campaign process was particularly awkward

13. Graham and Godfrey, "If These Allegations Are True."

and troubling, and a lot of intentionally religious imagery was used by Moore and his supporters. As in the previous example, people were left scratching their heads as to how someone with such clear dissonance between his personal actions and his alleged faith could be found morally acceptable by the vast majority of evangelical voters. The simple answer I would give to this conundrum is that the United States is deeply entrenched in civil religion, wherein the lines between church and state have been so blurred as to be almost unrecognizable. The faith that is growing in such a climate is often unhealthy, as we'll examine in the following chapter. Much of this is due to the rocky soil of civil religion.

Christianity has been intentionally co-opted by the state in ways that place civil allegiance above ecclesial fidelity and in such a way that most cannot distinguish between the two. For many if not most Christians that find themselves living in the United States, to be an "American" is to be a Christian, end of story. This is deeply problematic. Moreover, many have bought into the narrative that this identity is under attack by Democrats in particular, and so there is a strongly reactionary and fundamentalist response that sees the Republican Party as the only hope of the United States. As such, Christians buying into this scheme have proven themselves willing to vote for literally anyone so long as they claim to be Republican, regardless of their character. The hypocritical reality of this is clearly evident to those outside the cultic following of this schema, and people have had enough. It is also true that this civil religious viewpoint has become synonymous, for most, with Christianity itself. And so, the Christianity that we are left with in the United States is one whose allegiance is misplaced, and whose gospel is strangely out of line with the ways and teachings of Jesus. The general public is increasingly incredulous toward this reality and thus toward the church.

Chapter 4

FALSE WITNESS
Moral Therapeutic Deism

I AM A NOVICE farmer at best. I am fairly adept at keeping plants like succulents alive, and I enjoy having flowers around to beautify our yard and home. In our current home we have many fruit trees and I tend them as best I can, as I really enjoy their harvest. We also have a raised bed garden. I am less successful growing crops in this format. Some years are better than others. Once, as I prepared the beds in the spring and planted seeds, I sowed what I thought was a variety of crops: tomatoes, peppers, green beans, broccoli, and cucumbers. In reality, though, I planted marigold seeds in place of the broccoli seeds and ended up without any broccoli. The flowers certainly helped draw pests away from the vegetables, but they were not what I was intending to grow. My intentions were good, but I planted the entirely wrong crop.

Practical theologian Kendra Creasy Dean, leaning on the work of sociologists of religion Christian Smith and Melina Lundquist Denton, has suggested that the church has committed the same error as I did, albeit on a much grander scale.[1] In short, rather than planting seeds of authentic orthodox Christianity, the church has opted for the much faster growing, but less biblical or creedal, seeds of moral therapeutic deism. Dean calls the adherents of such

1. See Dean, *Almost Christian*, and Smith and Denton, *Soul Searching*.

faith "Almost Christians," borrowing from a phrase and sermon title used by both George Whitefield and John Wesley during the period known as the Great Awakening, in the mid-eighteenth century. Such "Christians," notes Dean, have not fully committed their lives to Christ and do not fully believe the gospel, and all of this because they haven't really been given a chance. Rather than being offered the difficult, divisive, and downright strange gospel, they were instead sold (see the next chapter) a watered-down version of Christianity that focused on generalized moral teachings on which all can agree. The targeted result of such "evangelism" is usually a better, more successful life, all framed by the belief in a benevolent God, usually devoid of the scandalous particularity of the cross, to borrow a helpful phrase from Søren Kierkegaard. Dean's focus is on understanding the faith of American teenagers, and hopefully discipling them in the ways of authentic Christianity. Since its release in 2010 I have maintained that *Almost Christian* should be required reading for all clergy, with the scope of the target audience being widened from youth to most all Christians in America. I believe, after all, that we have been sowing these seeds for a long time. Today this alternative gospel is incredibly "successful." It is the message that Joel Osteen preaches to around seven million people each week. It is the message of most Hollywood films that dare to encroach upon the subject of (Christian) faith. In many ways, this is the same message proclaimed by people like Oprah, and it's also the same watered-down, generalized version of Christianity held and proclaimed by most American politicians—be they on the "Left" or "Right." Jimmy Carter is one key outlier in this regard, and he was probably one of the most unpopular US presidents of all time. Moral therapeutic deism (hereafter MTD) is bland, lukewarm, watered down, easy to swallow, unoffensive, unspecific, safe, tame, and carefully regulated in order to reach the highest number of people as possible. The authentic biblical and creedal gospel, on the other hand, is offensive, scandalous, off-putting, particular, risky, demanding, wild, hot or cold, and all-consuming. As Dietrich Bonhoeffer noted in his hugely important work *Discipleship*, the call of the gospel is the call to come and die. This is not, and never will be, a popular message—but it is nonetheless true.

Why have so many swapped out the gospel for MTD? The powerful theological aesthetics of Roman Catholic theologian Hans Urs von Balthasar testifies time and again to the idea that the useful has destroyed the beautiful in the modern world. Balthasar was, I believe, responding to a quote from Victor Hugo's monumental work *Les Misérables*: "The beautiful is just as useful as the useful. Perhaps more so."[2] For both Hugo and Balthasar, "the beautiful" refers to that which is right, and true, and good, and is likewise an aesthetic reference that to which is ultimately all goodness, truth, and beauty: God. That which is right, and true, and good is not always what is easy, useful, or productive. This is a conundrum that takes center stage in modernity/postmodernity, and most would conclude that usefulness or utility has been deemed more important than beauty (or truth or goodness for that matter).

In a similar way, philosopher Alisdair MacIntyre has suggested that one of the key tensions between the ancient (especially Greek) world and the modern world is that of excellence versus efficiency.[3] MacIntyre suggests that the ancient Greeks, with their focus on virtue, valued excellence above all else, whereas the rise of modernity and especially the Industrial Revolution saw a shift away from excellence toward efficiency. In other words, what is now deemed most important is that which can produce the most of something in the fastest and easiest manner possible. This is seen in handmade versus machine-made products, organic versus GMO crops, and even online versus in-person learning. In every way imaginable, most people and societies have opted for efficiency and utility over and against excellence and beauty.

The church is guilty of this just as much as corporations, marketplaces, and societies. More and more "viewers" watch "church" happen on a screen at home, on their device, or at satellite campuses of large megachurches. Christian imagery is often missing from places of worship, sacraments not received, community not

2. Hugo, *Les Misérables*, I.21.
3. MacIntyre, *After Virtue*.

built. People come and go, receiving a fifty-five-minute dose of "Christianity" aimed at motivating people to be happier, healthier, and to keep people coming, all in time for the next service to begin. Professional music leaders write new songs each week, expressing emotivism aimed at authenticity, but lacking the rich depth of the great hymns. Large-budget ministry groups plan enormous events aimed at spreading the message of MTD, usually to a recycled audience of Christians who attend other, smaller churches nearby. Visitors hope to win a new car giveaway, watch as Easter eggs are dropped from helicopters, and adore local and global celebrities with little to no theological training standing in as guest speakers. And regardless of the scale of one's worship experiences, the messages received typically do not challenge believers to repent and change, but to self-care, and to seek personal happiness. If "the world" is challenged in any way, it is usually only a particular political party (typically, but not always, the Democratic Party), with the understanding that we just need to have the right governmental leaders (usually assumed to be Republicans) in charge for all to be well (see chapter 3). A decade or two ago, the above-mentioned tactics would often take place at evangelistic "crusades," so named as an intentional whitewashing of the tactics of the church hundreds of years ago when the gospel was spread by force via the colonizing agents of Europe. The goal then, as now, was simply to gain converts—regardless of the tactics. The ends justified the means. Again, this has been going on for a long time— the tactics may change, but the root problem remains. The church has mistakenly accepted the premise that bigger is better, more is best, and that however the "gospel" is spread, the end results are all that matters. For hundreds of years we deluded ourselves into thinking that things were working. We can no longer abide such delusions, however. People have left and are leaving the church in countless droves and, as Dean suggests, we are responsible. The gospel we gave (or sold) to them, the gospel of MTD, is not deep or substantial enough to handle real-life woes, real suffering, doubts, or even the cultural pressure being placed upon the church by its despisers. The gospel of MTD has been found wanting and it is being discarded at a record pace. Most are leaving and never looking back.

Why wouldn't they leave? I don't expect to win any popularity contests with this, but the message that so many of us have been peddling for so long, the message of MTD, is non-compelling and ultimately unhelpful. I think people are right to leave the church if this is our message. Sure the ready-made packaging is easy to handle, but the contents of the message do not truly satisfy. MTD is like a lunchable compared to a home-cooked, three-course meal! The food in the lunchable—if it can actually be considered *real* food—is bland, unsatisfying, and not all that filling. A homemade meal, on the other hand, requires so much more work, but the food itself, as well as the fellowship of friends and family sharing such a meal, provides sustenance for a long time.

There are so many simple, everyday examples of the gospel of MTD. Recently I attended a graveside service for a wonderful Christian man. The service was conducted by a military chaplain, but it was clear that the deceased was a Christian. I noted with great sadness that the term "resurrection" was not mentioned once in what he shared. In fact, almost nothing about faith, and certainly nothing that was specifically Christian, was mentioned. Resurrection—the great hope of the Christian faith according to Paul in 1 Corinthians 15—ought to be named and proclaimed at the burial of a Christian. If not, what are we doing? Yes, resurrection is weird, it is unscientific, unobservable, challenging to accept, and illogical to some, and yet it is the very heart of the gospel. If we shirk this message for a bland, warmed over message of death, God's love, and the promise that "we'll be together soon," then has anything truly Christian happened? Could the same words not be applied to a person of any faith, as well as a secular person who was at least agnostic in some way, or whose surviving family is? There is no better time than a funeral, and especially a graveside service, to proclaim the strange hope of the gospel, that death has lost its ultimate grip over us because of the life, death, resurrection, and ascension of our Lord and Savior Jesus Christ. We are to proclaim this message to comfort the living, and because for millennia, these words have been prophetically and defiantly proclaimed as truth of that which lies ahead for both our loved ones and for ourselves if we will place our trust and faith in the Lord Jesus.

I recall another example of MTD replacing the gospel from my days of coursework for my PhD at a United Methodist Seminary. The school decided to host an art exhibit (which I think is a cool idea) titled "Faces of God." Unfortunately, though, many of the faces of God displayed were definitely non-Christian images. One image in particular was of Kali the destroyer, from Hinduism. I remember thinking this was an odd thing to display in a seminary whose primary task is to train women and men for full-time pastoral ministry. I make this observation over and against a religion department in a large university, where such religious diversity would be welcome and expected. This unfortunate choice was made all the more tragic when a master's student from South Asia protested the image's presence on the grounds that his grandparents were chased from their homes back in India and killed by Hindu extremists, who elevated the image of Kali the destroyer. Even in receiving this formal complaint, the seminary elected to preserve the exhibit and the Kali piece in the name of religious tolerance and diversity. That a Christian seminary would rather promote religious tolerance and diversity than accommodate the faithful request of a persecuted Christian speaks loads for what MTD is all about. At the end of the day the specificity of the gospel is eschewed for a more generalized faith. This student's experience was unfortunate, but it was more important that the school be tolerant of the artist and her work. The message was clear, and it was a message I saw clearly imparted on the MDiv students: proclaim God in whatever form you wish, but do not do so in a way that excludes one image over and against another. MTD does not necessarily lead to religious pluralism as demonstrated here, but it is difficult to demonstrate why it shouldn't. The decision made by the school was a pragmatic one in that it ensured that the most people were appeased. I do not know how this decision finally played itself out in terms of this man from India's faith, but I can't imagine it was helpful. There are so many examples of MTD from my own personal experiences. My hunch is that you don't have to look far for practical examples of the gospel of Jesus (including the strangeness of his birth, his death, and especially his resurrection and ascension, along with the call to holy living) being replaced by a more generalized, easy to accept, but less dynamically life-changing message. That message, the message of MTD, is ultimately the simple proclamation that there is a God who is good who wants you to feel good about yourself. Moreover, such sermons typically feature a how-to or self-help focus aimed at being practically beneficial to one's everyday life.[4] Surely there is more to the gospel than this?!

I think it's also true that the reaction against MTD reveals a difficult truth about the gospel, but one that is evident in Scripture. Namely, that the true path of discipleship is narrow, winding, and difficult compared to the broad, straight, easy pathway of the world. Maybe the church is not supposed to be so large? Maybe salvation lies beyond the walls of the church, and thankfully we are not meant to sort that out. Perhaps it is possible that, as Stanley Hauerwas has so pointedly taught, it is necessary for the church to be the church so that the world can actually know itself as the world.[5] If the church is to be an alternative community, then it must be just that: an alternative to something else. In this case, the church is the alternative to the world.

Finally, I think it is important to point out that the gospel of MTD is not the gospel being proclaimed in most of the rest of the world currently, especially not in the southern hemisphere, where Christianity is growing exponentially. I recognize that this is a dangerously generalized statement, but there, in the southern hemisphere, the gospel is being proclaimed, in many instances to those with nothing and not in a way that promises to make their lives better. Instead, the numbers of believers is growing because the gospel is being proclaimed and then people are experiencing the goodness and grace of God in community. Lives are being

---

4. As opposed to the proclamation of what God has done, is doing, and will do and the need to orient our lives around this good news.

5. Hauerwas, "Reforming Christian Social Ethics."

changed, resulting in faithful Christian witness. The church is being lifted up in contrast to the world and the result is staggering.

The current exodus of people away from the church and all things related to Christianity is not solely the result of the sowing of the seeds of MTD, but I do believe this is one of key components in this reality. People leave because they think Christians are too judgmental. They leave because we have outdated sexual ethics. They leave because we are not relevant. They leave because we are too tied to corrupt politicians and parties. They leave because we are not diverse. They leave because we want their money. They leave because we dare to tell people right and wrong, or to offer advice on how people should and should not live. They leave because pro sports, Little League, traveling teams, birthday parties, brunches, Costco, and so many other things are more enticing on Sunday mornings. They leave because they are tired from working long hours, commuting in and out of the city, never seeing their children, and they just don't want one more commitment. People leave for all these reasons and more. Deep down, though, my suspicion is that the number one reason why people leave and stay away is that they are bored. They don't believe because they have not been captured by the awesome love and wonder of the gospel of the God who would create all, despite the reality that creation would choose sin over its Creator, and who would then would go to the extent of the cross to win us back, redeem the world, and adopt us into God's very own household and family. The leave because they have not truly experienced the terrific mystery of the sacraments. They leave because the gospel has not truly been preached, and certainly hasn't been lived. They leave because lost in the production of church they were never invited in to it all, as participants. They leave because they are seeds that never took root in the rocky, poisoned soil and so have withered and died. They have left, are leaving, and likely will not come back not because their ears were deaf, but because we gave them something utterly unsatisfying, uncaptivating, and in the end, unfaithful. They leave because they have not truly come to know, love, and serve Jesus and that responsibility falls almost solely on us, you, and in particular, me. As a full-time pastor I accept responsibility for my share of this problem. In part 2 of this book, I'll offer thoughts on how we might move forward in a corrective manner.

Chapter 5

STUNTED GROWTH

Consumerism

GROWING PLANTS, EVEN IN the most ideal circumstances, can be a truly difficult task. Good soil, favorable weather conditions, and even good seeds can all be thwarted by unwanted toxins being introduced into the soil or directly onto the plants themselves. Accidentally spilling something like gasoline, or the incautious use of pesticides too close to plants you want to protect, can wind up killing a plant that ought to survive and even thrive. To continue with the example I have utilized over the last few chapters, it has to be admitted that while seeds technically possess everything they need in order to grow, their success can easily be thwarted by a number of factors, like the ones explored in the preceding chapters. In this chapter I will suggest that, in terms of the working metaphor, our best efforts at growth are being thwarted by poison being consistently thrown onto our plants and soil. Sometimes we are guilty of unwittingly exposing our plants to this poison, and sometimes the poison comes from outside forces. The poison that I am referring to is the poison on consumerism. It is true that in many ways this poison is inescapable in our modern (and especially Western) world, but it should be possible to limit our exposure. Instead, the church typically is guilty of self-contamination, as we naively assume that we can harness the power of consumerism without ourselves being consumed.

As a teenager I was a part of youth ministries whose leaders liked to periodically encourage the teens to destroy their secular music, and only listen to "Christian" contemporary music. I must admit that I did this on two different occasions. Soon after both foolish endeavors, I attempted to rebuild my collection through Columbia House's mail-in CD club. Some of what these leaders were encouraging us was good: what I was listening to did matter and it did shape and form me. The language, values, and culture of such music is powerfully formative. This is still something I pay attention to today, and I think it's something we all should be aware of. Some things are just not good for us. And yet the church has an ancient tradition of plundering the Egyptians, especially in terms of art. I believe that sometimes (not always), secular or vulgar art can serve as avenues to ponder the human condition or God's goodness or some other subject in a way that an intentionally "Christian" substitution might not. As a theologian and pastor I could go on about this at length. For now, though, let me simply suggest that this is an issue where discipleship, sensitivity to the Holy Spirit, confession, and accountability are all key. I do not believe there is or should be a hard and fast rule against secular art, while at the same time I recognize that some secular art, even the most innocuous, can be, for some, idolatrous and destructive.

My concern in this chapter, though, is that what my pastors and peers did not notice is that while the content of our music was being scrutinized, our fundamentally ascribed role as consumers was only being fed through the exercise of destroying "secular" music and replacing it with "Christian" music. During this period, it was extremely common to hear Christian musicians identify themselves as the Christian version of a particular secular artist. If you liked Pearl Jam, then you might like Third Day. Or, if you liked the Red Hot Chili Peppers you could purchase Audio Adrenaline instead. Those who got rid of their Eminem CDs could purchase the work of KJ-52. Fans of boy bands could purchase Plus One rather than NSYNC or the Backstreet Boys. Artistically, there is so much to critique about this: what sort of artist sets out to be just like someone else but with slightly different lyrics? Interestingly enough, though, it worked. The Christian music industry became a major market in the 1990s thanks to this copycat approach. I'm confident that some embraced this route evangelistically. Others, though, surely approached this from a purely business perspective.[1] It cannot be debated that this business model was one focused on success in terms of sales by the record company executives—just like the secular record companies. In fact, I can't help but wonder if the assumption by the entertainment industry as a whole all along was that we Christians would simply end up buying both types of music, and thus consume even more! This is certainly what many of my friends and I did.

This process cemented a business model that has grown exponentially for Christian artists across many different genres of art and entertainment, including music, motion pictures, and written works of fiction and nonfiction. Fast forward to today and enter the world of social media "influencers," coffee shops in megachurches, and the very big business that worship has become around the world. Large churches, almost always, grow and remain large based upon a business model that entails a lot of strategic spending on areas such as marketing, music, and children's ministry/entertainment. Christian authors buy into a scheme to endlessly promote their "brand," following a pipeline from social media, to blogs, podcasts, then books, and then, for the super successful, lucrative speaking engagements. Seminary or post-graduate education is rarely required for such popular pundits of faith—in fact it is typically a hindrance to their success. In short, Christian entertainment in its various forms has become big business. Those who desire to compete in this market are almost always required to sell themselves (and I mean this fairly literally) in order to succeed.[2]

1. I still remember how sad I was when I learned of some of the things my friends who went to school in Nashville saw from many big name allegedly "Christian" musicians in terms of alcohol, drugs, and even sex around the Music Row area. The contemporary example of comedian John Crist is a sad illustration of this same phenomenon.

2. I readily acknowledge the inherent tension in these comments: I am a Christian author writing a book you had to purchase. For what it is worth, I do have an earned PhD, do not sell many books, do not want to become a Christian "influencer," and refuse to publish with a company that would require me

I describe this thoroughly Western phenomenon as hyper-consumeristic Christianity. This phenomenon has had a devastating impact on the church. It is extremely difficult for a small church to grow today without money. In particular, without money to spend on highly professionalized music and media, large growth is almost impossible. Today worship teams are expected to be large, diverse, young, and incredibly talented to the point of consistently writing their own original songs (lyrics and music). Australia's Hillsong or California's Bethel Church are seen as guides in this new way of worship. Bible studies are increasingly seen as "old-fashioned" compared to hip and relevant purchase-and-play video series by uber-famous Christian influencers. Many churches are actually satellite campuses of larger churches, where people go, sit, watch, and worship under the leadership of a megachurch but in their own neighborhood. In such churches, it's common to have a campus pastor who helps facilitate the worship experience for attenders. Some such churches watch and sing along with worship music on the screen from the mother church, whereas some employ local musicians for music, but then watch the pastor's sermon on a movie-theatre-like large screen. @ChurchHome in the Seattle area (and now Los Angeles) is seen as a prime example for this new wave of churchgoing.[3] This new model for doing church has its benefits and its drawbacks. For the purposes of this book, I am simply suggesting that such methods of worship commodify and then franchise worship in convenient locations much like another Seattle-based consumer giant: Starbucks. These new megachurches perfectly blend together the experience of a concert, a movie, Christian teaching, and all in very nice facilities with outstanding coffee and top-notch child care. As churches like @ChurchHome grow and spread out their franchises or satellite campuses, it is increasingly difficult for regular, smaller, parish

---

to enter into this aforementioned scheme.

3. It's worth noting that churches like @ChurchHome depend largely on large embodied gatherings at various locations rather than at-home viewing such as was common in the '80s and '90s and which came to a climax with the ministry of Joel Osteen. Pastor Judah Smith is able to preach to thousands across the world through various satellite campuses or online services.

congregations to survive. Who can compete, after all, with the talent level, marketing, financial infrastructure, and accessibility of such large multi-site churches?

This book is not necessarily a critique of churches like @ChurchHome, although certainly the content of the last few chapters ought to be brought to bear on this model. Instead, the reason to bring up these new models of church is that they are the logical development of the hyper-consumerism of Christianity. For good or for bad, such churches will likely always thrive. The question, is, at what cost? Are we, like Neil Postman has suggested about Western culture as a whole, amusing ourselves to death?[4]

We have come a long way from Jesus overturning the tables of the money changers in the temple in Matthew 21:12–13. There, Jesus was not upset about money being present or exchanged in the temple. We must not oversimplify this complex passage. Instead, Jesus was upset that the poor and the Gentiles in particular, who were attempting to worship the God of Israel, were being financially taken advantage of. This was not the point of the sacrificial system and Jesus was furious that these people were being robbed in the name of his Father. Elsewhere we learn that Jesus and his disciples benefitted from the charitable giving of several women, namely Joanna, wife of Chusa, who was Herod's administrator.[5] Thus not only did Jesus receive money from wealthy women for his ministry, but some of this money came from someone who worked for Herod! Money is not inherently evil—it is not inherently anything as a matter of fact. It can be, though, the root of all evil, if and when it commodifies things and people. Perhaps more importantly, money, and the love of it, has the ability to re-narrate the world according to its own terms so that we humans become valued based upon how much money we have, how we use it, our ability to acquire it, etc. This is what has happened in the modern, market-driven world we live in. Money has been reified with the result that everything else has become commodified.

4. Postman, *Amusing Ourselves to Death*.
5. Luke 8:1–3.

As churches have grown more and more professional, the church has experienced this as well. Churches and individual Christians are consumers like everyone else. In fact this is possibly the one classification that we cannot really escape in the world in which we live. Churches have become businesses. This was not intentional—or at least not always intentional. In this way the church of today is almost unrecognizable compared to the early church. Lest we be overly critical, though, we must remember that almost everything about the world in which we live is unrecognizable compared to the ancient world. Rather than take a stance for or against the institutional church (as a big business), I simply point out that this model is no longer faithfully sustainable for most of the church. Churches are building new buildings at much slower rate than ten to twenty years ago. Increasingly churches struggle under the burden of buildings that are too large to maintain—remnants of a period of dynamic numerical growth and economic optimism that is long gone. Pastors are receiving less and less pay, causing many to turn to bi-vocational or entrepreneurial ministry just to survive. Offerings and budgets steadily decline, as most reports claim that only about 2 percent of Christians tithe. The only exceptions to this, typically, are the sorts of churches discussed earlier in this chapter, where tithing levels are likely in line with these statistics but sheer numbers allows for a larger budget. Meanwhile, businesses require longer hours from their employees, commuting distances increase, children's extracurricular activities increase, and entertainment culture encroaches steadily on times and places that used to be sacred. As a result, Sunday morning is now a time slot full of options, as is Wednesday night. Sports events, and other forms of live-action entertainment are available to watch every night of the week, and shopping is always available—even to the person sitting in the pew on their digital device. Consumerism knows no bounds, the marketplace doesn't respect boundaries or borders, and the church is inescapably caught up in this—especially when it attempts to harness the power of the marketplace for the purpose of growth. As a great critic of Christianity famously wrote, "Whoever fights monsters should see to it that in the process he does not become a monster. And when you look long into an abyss, abyss also looks into you."[6] In the second half of this book I will suggest that the church of tomorrow—the resurrected church in the West—will need to embrace the role of an outpost of the kingdom of God amid the totalizing vision of the marketplace, and not as another of its franchises. We must be in and not of the world, in other words.

What I have tried to suggest in this chapter is that the church has often been guilty of passing itself off as just another consumer option, using marketing strategies in place of discipleship, with the express goal of enlarging its market or territory, i.e., growing numerically. As Stanley Hauerwas has oft suggested, though, the purpose of the church is not to grow, but rather to be faithful. We are guilty of making growth our goal, rather than the Spirit-provided byproduct of faithfulness. We have accepted the growth of previous centuries as the norm, and thus assumed that such growth should and will continue. In this we have failed to take into account the subject of previous chapters, and in particular, moral therapeutic deism. All things considered, the church is guilty of consumer fraud: selling one thing under the guise of something else.[7] Such tactics surely work for a while, but eventually this kind of business implodes upon itself. The interesting thing, in this case, is that the "product" we have to "sell" is of the utmost quality and literally sells itself. The only issue is that it is hard for many to accept this "product," i.e., the gospel, and thus it will never see the kind of exponential growth that (market) growth strategists want

---

6. Nietzsche, *Beyond Good and Evil*, 146.

7. Let me remind the reader that we are drawing to the close of the diagnostive portion of this book. I firmly believe in the gospel, its truth, God's desire to draw to God's self all people—all of creation even—and that ultimately all of creation will be redeemed. That said, I don't think the content of our popular message or the tactics utilized in disseminating it line up with the form and content of the true gospel. I think that our dependency upon the marketplace betrays a mistrust in the scandalously particular gospel. I am thus not critical of the gospel in any way, and I believe it will succeed, but not in the way we are currently going about proclaiming it.

to see from a successful business. Perhaps the gospel is a small-batch product, intended for a weirdly devoted, but small, market.

I will always remember my first Krispy Kreme donut. The year was 1998. On a trip to the Dallas are with friends to visit Six Flags Over Texas a friend told us about this donut place that we just had to try. "A donut place, at night?" I said. His answer was simple, "Yes." Apparently, many others had the same idea, because when we pulled up we were greeted with a drive-through line that could rival In-N-Out. When we finally made it through the line and I had my first "hot and fresh" Krispy Kreme, I was in love. A couple years later, a Krispy Kreme store opened in the Anaheim area near Crystal Cathedral (interesting parallel . . .) and I just had to go. Together with my fiancée and a couple friends, we departed our University in San Diego home around 10 p.m. for what would be the ultimate gold standard in late-night snack runs! Those donuts were simply amazing. Everybody else thought so too. Soon I began to notice boxes of Krispy Kremes in gas stations and grocery stores. Walmarts and Targets had Krispy Kreme donuts. Krispy Kreme stores were popping up everywhere. People were selling Krispy Kremes for fundraisers. In short, Krispy Kreme donuts were everywhere. These donuts didn't come "hot and fresh" and the market was simply oversaturated. They were no longer special. Again, I guess others felt the same. In 2004 market oversaturation and overexpansion as well as an SEC investigation into financial mismanagement caused the donut giant to falter. Market shares that began around $5 each and climbed to almost $45 each, plummeted to $12.75. Stores closed, donuts sat unpurchased, uneaten, and eventually became trash—a metaphor for the company as a whole. I know that personally I went about ten years without eating a Krispy Kreme or caring to, but still I remembered the amazing "hot and fresh" donuts coming right off the conveyer belts at the stores.

What happened? Did the donuts change? No. Instead, the management, delivery, and business model of Krispy Kreme changed and as a result, the company nearly died. It's fascinating to me that a company with such an amazingly delicious and simple product could rise so quickly and fall even quicker all due to mismanagement and a poor business model. You see, Krispy Kreme forgot something very important: if a person simply wanted a donut, they could get one anywhere. If they wanted a Krispy Kreme, though, and if they wanted it "hot and fresh," they had to go directly to the source. People didn't want cheap, easy-to-obtain, and likely stale donuts, they wanted the experience of having a Krispy Kreme donut. Today Krispy Kreme has rebounded, though they will likely never be as big as they were in the early 2000s. They acknowledge that their products don't really lend themselves to exponential growth. If nothing else, the donuts simply don't stay fresh long enough. As they have cautiously re-expanded, they have self-imposed limits, they are much more selective of their locations, their stores are smaller, and they're attempting to also capitalize on the ever-expanding market for coffee in the United States and around the world. They are consistent in their focus, though. Krispy Kreme leaders left no stone unturned as they attempted to turn around their faltering company. One thing they didn't have to change, though, was the donuts. "We inherited an incredible brand," one leader said.[8] What Krispy Kreme has learned is that they do not need to sell the fresh donuts—they sell themselves. Instead, they simply need to be more realistic about the size of the market such a product can realistically reach without compromising its integrity.

Does the church have the courage to learn from Krispy Kreme? My hope is to offer some thoughts on just that in the second half of this book. For now, though, our numbers are dropping rapidly, trust in our brand is all but dried up, and we are under constant scrutiny from both outside and inside for financial and sexual misconduct. A change is surely needed.

8. Kowitt, "Behind the Krispy Kreme Turnaround."

Chapter 6

A CONCLUSION OF SORTS

What Happens When They Leave?

RECALLING SOME OF THE work done in chapter 2, roughly one in four attend a Christian worship service somewhat regularly in the United States. Recent statistics reveal that where I currently live and pastor, the San Francisco Bay Area, the number of people that actually attend a Christian worship service regularly is as low as 3 percent. Church attendance at both the local and national levels continues to decline rapidly for almost all major churches. A recent Gallup study quantifies this decline at nearly 20 percent over the past twenty years.[1] Small to medium-sized churches seem to be the worst off as they find themselves increasingly unable to compete with megachurches and their aesthetically pleasing buildings and highly professionalized music and children's ministries. The climate of the church in North America has largely given way to a sense of panic-induced desperation. Lost amid empire, bad theology, lost mission, and the all-consuming marketplace, we are desperate for anything that offers results. We have the best intentions: we want the church to be relevant and large and we want people to know and believe in the gospel. But you know what they say about good intentions . . .

1. Jones, "U.S. Church Membership Down Sharply."

54

Is the opening image of old, somewhat crazy Luke Skywalker starting to make sense yet? Perhaps, like Luke says, it's time to let the church, like the Jedi, die. But wait, the story doesn't end there! If you'll recall, the Jedi do not die off, in fact they rise again! No longer, though, will they be the puppets of the empire. No longer will they be "mainstream." Instead, they will be an ancient and most peculiar religion, unapologetically so. In the character of Rey, Luke realizes that the Jedi order will always live on, but it's beyond his control. And, as the film ends, we see a little boy, who happens to be a force-wielder, dreaming and gazing into the stars. The force will not ever cease to be, nor will there cease to be those who are sensitive to it. It is much the same with the gospel. It will always be, for it is the very fabric of the universe. The kingdom it proclaims is coming, indeed it has drawn near, and it will have no end. There will always be those that are sensitive to it, and hopefully that number will grow and grow until God is all in all—but that is likely a long way off. What's more, this growth is solely in the hands of God the Almighty, whose Holy Spirit preveniently gathers creation toward himself, and not the result of our growth strategies or tactics. Christ-followers are not market analysts or growth strategists, but disciples—faithfully living out the ways of Jesus in and for the world. Disciples, by virtue of being disciples, make other disciples—the Holy Spirit ensures this. In this way the gates of hell will never prevail against the church. In order for this to happen, though, the church must get out of its own way. I think it's time to respond to the call of Christ to "come and die," as Dietrich Bonhoeffer said. The same can surely be said for the church as well.

In Romans 6, the Apostle Paul lays out the definitive theology for Christian baptism. In particular Paul says,

> Do you not know that all of us who have been baptized into Christ Jesus were baptized into his death? Therefore we have been buried with him by baptism into death, so that, just as Christ was raised from the dead by the glory of the Father, so too might we walk in newness of life.[2]

2. Rom 6:3–4. Indeed the whole chapter is worth considering as it so

According to Romans 6, when a person is baptized in the name of the Father, the Son, and the Holy Spirit, they are believed to have died—their "old self" anyway, and a new person has risen out of the waters with Christ by the power of the Holy Spirit. For this reason the early church used to baptize converts without any clothes, and then thrust new white robes on them when they emerged from the waters, new women and men, adopted into the household of God, filled with the Holy Spirit. Baptismal dates even became more important than birth dates for many. In baptism, the God of resurrection, the God who makes all things new, was doing something new in their lives and in the world. Behold, the old had passed away, and the new had come.[3] But in order for that new to come, in order for resurrection to occur, death was required. The call to die was also a call to be reborn. But it was, first and foremost, a call to die. To follow Christ is to die a thousand different deaths in one before it is to be reborn and renewed. We all must die if we are to follow Christ. Why should it not be the same for the church? I believe this is where we are in North America. Like the Great Barrier Reef, the church is dying, and in some places it is dead already. It is a complex organism containing both life and death, but significantly trending in the direction of death. So what? Maybe this is not as terrible as it sounds. Perhaps this is simply one step on the way of discipleship. Perhaps our institutions, like ourselves, must die, in order to be reborn. Perhaps we should take our cue from Isaiah's theme of resurrection amid Babylonian captivity found especially in Isaiah 40–55. Death and resurrection has always been a part of the story of the people of God. God has done a new thing before, and in fact is still working that new thing to fulfillment.[4]

---

powerfully conveys the gospel and what, in particular, happens in Christian baptism.

3. 2 Cor 5:17.

4. Many thanks to my good friend and colleague Rev. David Steinhart for this reminder and many good reminders and comments in reading through this manuscript.

Yes, the church is dying. I do not think we need to concern ourselves with saving it. Instead, let us embrace this opportunity for intense discipleship, and look for the signs of new resurrection life that God will inevitably bring all around us. Perhaps such new resurrection life is already stirring.

PART II

The Resurrection of the Church in North America

Chapter 7

WHAT ARE WE LEFT WITH?

NEW LIFE IS STIRRING amid the rubble. If you made it through the first half of this book, you are either a glutton for punishment and bad news, or else you are radically optimistic about God's grace for the church. To avoid any misunderstandings, let me declare up front that I am profoundly persuaded of the latter. God has a plan for the church—that is the good news. The bad news, apparently, is that God's plan appears to be a bit different from ours—or at least from the late modern plans for a large, centralized, respectable institution alongside of other large, multinational institutions. People have left, and are leaving, the church in record numbers.

As I write this book I am the proud pastor of a small church in the Bay Area of Northern California. On a good Sunday, my church averages about seventy-five people, making us a pretty large church for this area! That number is down from over a hundred a few years ago, and down from around one thousand a couple decades ago (I know what you're thinking . . . the church was about the same size it is currently when I took over three years ago!). Beyond the stark drop in attendance, our church can boast of a very diverse congregation, an equally diverse church board, half of which are under forty, and a large and healthy lay-led compassionate ministry to those in need. Our per capita giving is good, the people care for and respect me as their pastor, and they're quick to respond to needs. Behind the seemingly negative numbers, therefore, is a story, one of loss, grief, and also of a good and healthy sense of vision and mission. Our story is indicative of so many churches in our area—indeed I think our story might be a bit better than average. We have poor numbers, but a great congregation. What if we attempted to look beyond the "poor numbers" of so many of our churches and instead listened to and observed their great stories? What if churches with supposedly "poor numbers" reimagined and refocused themselves around a new narrative of growth and opportunity—one not focused on large, dynamic, numerical growth, but rather on faithfulness and the construction of creative connections with the surrounding secular culture?

This is exactly what I want to suggest in the second half of this book. My main point is that what at first seems like death, is really the beginning of resurrection. I believe that smaller numbers do not equal a less healthy and effective church. Similarly, fewer full-time salaried clergy, and less denominational administration does not result in an unhealthy or doomed church. To the contrary, I believe these and many other challenges are opportunities for faithful re-creation and resurrection. This is a challenge that we know the Holy Spirit to be up for. God is always making things new, after all—and there is no reason to think this would not include the church!

In what follows, then, I will attempt to spin the negative numbers and observations from the first section into opportunities for positive ecclesial re-creation and resurrection. I will attempt to provide concrete examples and/or ideas about how the church can face down the challenges bearing down on it, while looking into a bright new tomorrow. In part 2 I will embrace the seeming death of the church as the very means by which God will resurrect the church. First, I will propose that the future of the church in North America will look much more like the first few centuries of the church's existence than the last seventeen centuries or so. In other words, the future of the church in North America is as a missionary movement of small, authentic communities stripped of much of the structure that has come to define the contemporary church:

large buildings, large paid staffs, and elaborate programized ministries. The future of the church in North America is small, communal, countercultural, and, I think, much more authentic. This
future, I'm convinced, will be a global future. The only chance
for a healthy church in North America is to remove any vestiges
of civil religion, to drop the partisan politics, and to live into the
countercultural political reality of the Lamb. As the church stops
seeking economic and political power, the church will stop being
beholden to political parties, businesses, and even the economy.
Letting go of the political (partisan on both sides) aspirations of
the state, we will be afforded the opportunity to again discover
and embody the politics of Jesus and his peaceable community.
Next, in chapter 9 we will consider the ramifications of moving
beyond the watered-down false gospel that is moral therapeutic
deism in favor of the rich, bold, and transformative gospel of Jesus
Christ. In worrying less about trying to please the largest number
of people possible, the church will rediscover the opportunity to
proclaim the scandal of the gospel to those willing to listen and respond. In this way the church should become known, once more,
for practicing what it preaches. In chapter 10, we will examine the
notion of "small-batch faith," wherein we acknowledge that we
cannot escape the marketplace, but that we can be more faithful
and creative stewards of that which we have been given. In no longer playing by the rules of the marketplace, the church will find
that it has the opportunity, once more, to shape its own strategies
and goals, rather than modeling them on the business world. And
finally, in chapter 11 we will look ahead to the potential landscape
of the church in the near future in North America. That future
will be populated with many, and diverse, smaller congregations
of Christians that look very different from the church of today, but
which desperately and faithfully cling to the gospel. And finally,
I will argue that the alleged "end" of the church is nothing but a
new, Spirit-filled beginning for the church. The look of the twenty-
first-century-and-beyond church may be literally unthinkable to
us now, but its teachings and core values and practices ought to be
thoroughly distinguished by and continuous with what the church

has been about since its inception. There will be both radical continuity and discontinuity between the church of today and that of yesterday. We need not fear this, though, for the discontinuity will always pale in comparison to the continuity. We have proclaimed the same gospel for two thousand years, and with a little creative reimagining of our mission, we will continue to do the same for thousands of years to come.

In the first parts of this book, I repeatedly examined and critiqued the image of a seed having all that it needs on its own to grow. I have to confess, now, that I was a bit too harsh in my treatment of this metaphor. While I think my critiques are valid, I failed to account for one crucial act: it was a metaphor. The very nature of a metaphor is that it opens up levels of understanding by comparing a thing with another thing. In doing so, however, it also limits understanding.[1] Take the common and biblical statement that "God is love," for example. One would be foolish to attempt to critique this metaphor. God is love. And yet what love is, is somewhat different for all. For the person who grew up in a loving home, and who has experienced the joy of a healthy and happy marriage, love is a great description for God. What is love, though, for the victim of child or spousal abuse? What about the person who suffered severe neglect? What might love be for a victim of child slavery or human trafficking? The illustrations can be endless. For each person, love means something slightly different. As an ideal, then, God is love. Practically speaking, this might be a less-than-helpful illustration or metaphor. The same is true for the metaphor of the seed. If the focus for the metaphor is organic, then the metaphor breaks down. If, though, the focus is on the gospel, as I believe the metaphor was intended, then the metaphor works. When the focus is on the gospel, we must admit, along with the well-intentioned leader who used this image in the first place, that the gospel is self-sufficient. It possesses all it needs for growth. The gospel does not die if it falls on deaf or distracted ears. The gospel does not whither or spoil if it comes to a person or household that is unobservant, unresponsive, or hardened against it. The gospel

1. See Gunton, *Actuality of Atonement*.

is able to patiently wait for ages, until a person is finally open to it. When a person is open to the gospel, it can take root and begin to flourish in even the most inhospitable elements, in the hardest of hearts. This happens not because of something special about the recipient, or because of any work that they do, but because the grace of God in the presence of the Holy Spirit instantly provides all that is needed for the gospel to flourish and thrive. The gospel is the in-breaking reality of the kingdom of God; it is the goodness of God poured out and opened up for all of Creation always, everywhere, and forevermore, until God is all in all and things are on earth as they are in heaven. Nothing can stop this because the power behind the gospel is the very power that created, sustained, redeemed, and is working to renew and restore all of creation. This power cannot fail. Thus, whereas the organic metaphor of the seed breaks down because a seed is simply not self-sufficient, the theological metaphor works quite well, as the gospel truly provides its own conditions and means for growth.

Moving forward, I will be attempting to unravel the negative analysis of the first part of this book by examining how the same content, viewed theologically, can become elements of, and opportunities for, resurrection. New life is occurring in the church. New life will happen for the church, and for all of Creation through the church. In even the most starkly secular contexts the church is perfectly positioned to be an outpost of Trinitarian faith, hope, and love. My opinion is that numbers will be smaller, in many cases, but that the opportunity for faithful witness will only increase. The church may suffer defeats, even resembling death, but ultimately it will not and cannot truly die—for how can a resurrection community ever really die? I am convinced that as the church finds a new reality in North America in particular, it will do so as a faith-based and service-oriented small community. Increasingly, churches will be known for the services they offer, as nonprofit "businesses" that engender and build community. Churches will be (I hope!) integral elements within local communities despite being understood to hold to weird, archaic beliefs. My hope is that churches will become places of lived-out, or embodied, faith, hope, and love. Like the illustration of the Jedi from the first part of this book, the future of the church in North America will likely be that of a small, peculiar, and yet extremely important and helpful religious group, whose strange religious beliefs will be tolerated, albeit begrudgingly, because of the services they offer to their surrounding communities.

In this way, the church will patiently witness to the gospel, the source and subject of its love for its community. Christianity is a religion—this is unavoidable. As I've defined it, a religion is a theory or set of beliefs commonly adhered to, about things such as the origin of all things, the divine, and the purpose of life. As the church adapts to its new reality it will learn to embody these beliefs to the public, while unashamedly teaching these beliefs to those who want to learn more about the God revealed in Jesus by the power of the Holy Spirit.

Chapter 8

WITNESS

The Politics of Jesus

IN CHAPTER 3 WE saw the crumbling away of the visible witness of the church in North America, but especially the United States, as it has so visibly aligned itself with certain political parties, candidates, and agendas. In particular, such alignment has been difficult to understand and embrace by younger people who find themselves confused by the dissonance between the values they were taught by their parents and teachers and the values displayed by the political parties and leaders now endorsed by those same parents and teachers. Sadly, through considering the role of civil religion, we saw that the issue is not one of mere endorsement, but one of confused allegiance between the kingdom of God and the kingdoms of this world. It is my opinion that this issue, more than anything else (at least in the United States) has sped up the rate of young people leaving the church to an almost unimaginable rate. This diagnosis is bleak, but resurrection can come in and through this situation. In this chapter we will consider ways that the church can forge ahead, outside of the relationship of civil religion, by embracing the politics of Jesus in a way that is both for and against the state.

If we were to quickly, and in an overly generalized manner, take stock of what we are left with as a church in North America

I think we'll see that we have a group of deeply divided people. Unfortunately, the lines of these divisions run parallel to the lines of division in broader culture. The church is divided between older, more conservative members and younger, more progressive members. The former group makes up the clear majority, but the latter is increasingly vocal about their desire to shape and lead into the future. This group recognizes that they have stayed despite so many others who have left and they want to be agents of change. Unfortunately, this divide often mirrors the divide between political parties in the United States as well: Republican and Democratic. Lest we continue with system of civil religion and simply swap out one party's hat or pendant for the other's, I suggest we strive for a much more complicated, but faithful, middle way. There is a long-standing tradition of this *via media* or middle way in the church. John Wesley was a prominent figure in this movement. In fact, the tradition of *via media* can be traced all the way back to Aristotle's virtue ethics, for which to be truly virtuous was the achievement of a balanced way between various extreme options. I suggest that such a path, that of *via media*, focused on the pursuit of Jesus, even unto the cross, is the political path the church is to tread if we are to safely move beyond civil religion.

Yes, the path ahead is political. Moving beyond civil religion and the current political quagmire the church finds itself in is neither a matter of swapping one set of (conservative) politics for another set of (progressive), nor is it a matter of becoming apolitical. No, for the church to move forward in this predicament, it must embrace the politics of Christian witness both for and against the nations. Despite his significant moral failures, John Howard Yoder's work in this area continues to serve as a helpful guide in embracing the politics of Jesus.[1] More recently, Bryan Stone's important book *Evangelism After Christendom* critically appropriates Yoder's work toward the purposes of developing a practical theology of evangelism in the post-Christendom world.[2] Stone's work is especially relevant to the present work, as he identifies North

1. Yoder, *Politics of Jesus.*
2. Stone, *Evangelism After Christendom.*

American civil religion as precisely that: a religion. His title is both accurate and also a bit of sleight of hand, as the primary other or competing religion Stone is concerned about over and against Christianity is North American civil religion. Stone claims, "If civil religion is a religion, however, it is probably the most influential and powerful of them because it is so pervasive."[3] This is an especially tricky scenario, in that civil religion in North America is a quasi-Christian religion that fails to see itself as *quasi* at all. In fact, it is far more appropriate to think of North American civil religion as a large heretical sect within the broader framework of orthodox Christianity. The early church would have most likely dealt with civil religion in this way. A council would have been convened, official teaching established, and a necessary fence would have been placed between orthodox Christianity and the quasi-Christianity of civil religion. This is extremely unlikely in the church today, though, which means that moving forward orthodox Christianity will have to learn how to confidently and boldly articulate itself over and against the heretical quasi-Christianity of civil religion.

Returning to Yoder via Stone, the key theme here is witness. We often understand witness, especially in Christian circles, as evangelistic proclamation. The term, though, derives from the Greek term *martyria* or "martyr." Witness, for the early church, was the faithfully embodied testimony to one's belief in Jesus Christ, even unto persecution and death. Witness is embodied or lived out faith. Christians have always been, and should always be, concerned about witness.

Another important term to parse is *political* or *politics*. Historically, speaking the term is much larger or broader than the way we often use it today. The term *politics* comes from the Greek word *polis*, which means city. To be political, therefore, is to live in a city or to live in community with others. As Aristotle claimed, we are social, or political, creatures. To be human, therefore, is to be political in that being human entails and requires that we navigate relationships with other humans. What's more, the church is specifically designated to be a group of people called out of the world

3. Stone, *Evangelism After Pluralism*, 56.

as a grafted-on extension of Israel, knit together into the body of Christ in and for the world.[4] As already mentioned, the church should neither swap one politics for another, nor should it attempt to be apolitical or nonpolitical. The church is deeply and inherently social or political, therefore. And so, the church is a social/political group focused on Christian witness—on embodied faithfulness to Christ—for the sake of the world. How the church lives, in other words, is what the church says it believes. The church is to embody the message it hopes others will believe.

It is probably time for some rebranding . . .

As the church moves forward it must acknowledge that it does so through a minefield of moral issues. This journey is made all the more precarious by the church's previous moral failures— most of which have been quite public in nature. Each step will need to be taken carefully, with constant and focused attention on Jesus, with an intentional goal of taking the middle way between the two extremes presented to us by our broader society. Instead of prescribing moral and political behaviors for others, what if the church confidently and patiently embodied its values in the model of Christian witness? For example, what if:

- The church was known for being peaceable and peacemaking?

- The church affirmed the sanctity of human life by opposing both abortion and capital punishment.

   » What if the church proactively worked to offer free options for women seeking abortions without passing judgment on those seeking abortion?

   » What if the church proactively worked to free those on death row and to reform the prison system?

- What if the church sought to love and serve aliens, orphans, and widows as outlined by the torah?

4. 1 Pet 2:9; Rom 11:17–31; 1 Cor 12:12–31.

- What if churches offered community garden space to community members dealing with food scarcity and poor access to fresh fruits and vegetables?

- What if churches offered after-school tutoring and social programs aimed at helping both students in need and working parents?

- What if churches banded together to offer co-op-style health assistance to members in need?

- What if churches were communities where young and old crossed generational and cultural divides to share meals, learn from one another, and worship together?

- What if church-based universities were determined to change the culture surrounding student loans and prevented clergy in particular from acquiring student loan debt?

- What if church communities were known for a particular product or service that they offered to the community in the name of Jesus?

  » Examples include a food bank, soup kitchen, nonprofit businesses that employed those in need of job skills training, free bike repair, laundromat, lawn care for elderly and disabled, and relocation assistance, and so forth.

- What if churches once again helped with the burial of members and loved ones, circumventing the complex and expensive secular industry that has grown up around death?

This limited list is just the beginning of reimagining the church in a way that is thoroughly political but outside the traditional reductionistic boundaries of North American civil religion. While some of these "what ifs" would benefit the United States, they would be acted upon for the sake of witnessing to the mission of the kingdom of God on earth as it is in heaven. Such practices are not utilitarian, nor are they aimed at the production of better citizens. Instead, such practices are sought to enhance fidelity to the mission of God as outlined in Scripture. Again, this way forward refuses to embrace left over right, or right over left, and it also does not strive to be apolitical. Instead, this approach is thoroughly political in that in aims at aiding and enhancing life in community. Such practices could take shape in a New Monastic Movement congregation, a house church, or an intentional traditional parish church in an urban or rural setting.

Ample empirical evidence suggests that the church in the United States has become so tied to partisan politics that people are leaving in droves.[5] The church, in short, has lost its credibility. The church is seen as justifying and endorsing unethical political candidates and parties—on both sides. The church seems more willing to support such candidates and parties than to support its Messiah who called his followers to care for the least of these and to pick up the cross and follow him. In many ways, the church has failed to live into Jesus' expectations, instead acquiescing to the more prevalent expectations of the nation state. What if we re-directed this political energy? What if the church, rather than endorsing political candidates and parties, focused on using the social/political passions of its members to enact change at the local level, such as the possibilities listed above? It's quite possible to transform what might be the church in North America's largest problem into a huge opportunity for growth and new life, or resurrection. All that is required to enact such change is creativity, hard work, and communal attentiveness to the gospel. Within the

5. There are, of course, exceptions. I maintain that while the future of the church in North America is small, there will always be megachurches, and many of these proudly proclaim a very politically charged message—either conservative or progressive. Indeed there are some that serve as cultural enclaves, rallying around a politically charged version of Christian faith. As culture continues to secularize, such enclaves will no doubt exist. I believe that these are the exceptions, though, and not the rule. Furthermore, they exist at the cost of peddling a slanted or skewed version of the gospel, pandering to only a particular demographic, and in such a way that only makes sense in light of current culture. In such cases, people are not necessarily being converted to the gospel, but are instead affirming each other against the progressive culture that surrounds them. As we have already seen, such "faith" usually does not last for it does not grow healthy, long-lasting roots.

church is enough money, education, and drive to enact amazing large and small-scale change worldwide, community by community. Can we do it?

Make no mistake about it, though, this is the largest and most difficult challenge facing the church. It is made all the more difficult in that almost no one recognizes it! Civil religion is a heretical, quasi-Christian religion, masquerading as orthodox Christian faith. Its adherents pastor churches, sit on every pew and around every church board table, they enter confession booths, work at soup kitchens, and volunteer at church work days. The task of pointing out the differences between orthodox Christianity and North American civil religion is a daunting one, fraught with peril, confusion, and possibly persecution. This is not a distinction that many want to make. And yet, for the integrity of the gospel and the church it calls out, this distinction must be made. Perhaps the best method of drawing such distinctions would be to return to our first love, as Jesus admonishes the church in Ephesus in Revelation 2. By returning to a strong, unapologetic focus on the gospel, we might find that on their own communities begin to rediscover their true, and thoroughly political, faith. In rediscovering and re-focusing on the gospel, it just might be that the church re-presents itself as a much-needed alternative to the divisive, unethical, and ultimately destructive gospel being preached by North American civil religion. For this reason, we will turn to a discussion of the gospel in the next chapter.

Chapter 9

PROCLAIMING THE TRUE GOSPEL

I OFTEN LIKE TO ponder this question: "What would happen if Jesus returned today, without any fanfare, and decided to visit churches around the world? How would he be welcomed? Would he be welcomed at all?" I suspect that he would not receive the welcome he deserves. I suppose this makes sense. Jesus has always been misunderstood and ill-received. Aside from the poor, women in particular, and a very small group made up of those from the rich and powerful portion of society, Jesus was often met with contempt and distrust. Why would it be any different today? I once asked author and pastor Alan Hirsch the question, "What do you think would happen if the church in North America encountered the real Jesus?" He responded that he was sad to say he thought about half of the church would probably leave in rejection of Jesus. I think Hirsch's response was spot on.

In chapter 4 we examined moral therapeutic deism (MTD), and saw that it subtly supplanted the authentic gospel of Jesus Christ as the primary message and evangelization tool used by the church in North America. With a different gospel being preached, one that is more convenient and user-friendly—one that asks less of us—it is no wonder why people have and continue to walk away from their faith in record numbers across North America. MTD is simply not robust enough to endure the real challenges of life and questions of theodicy. It's easy to be critical of MTD, and indeed we should be. We must also, though, recognize that MTD is not the true gospel. We must resist the temptation to camp out in critique, so to speak, rather than moving on toward the greener fields of the actual good news. At some point we must simply walk away from the false gospel of MTD toward the true gospel.

To return to the *Star Wars* analogy, MTD is the version of the Jedi that is beholden to the empire and their own power. But this is not the same as the teachings found in the ancient Jedi texts that Luke has been safeguarding, and which Rey takes and studies on her own. In these texts, Rey discovers the rich and strange teachings of the "hokey religion" that is the belief system of the Jedi.[1] The results of her study and discovery are essential for the ending of the Skywalker saga and the ultimate defeat the evil emperor. As I have already suggested, we must do the same thing if the church is to indeed prevail amid a world and culture characterized by contempt and the co-option of the gospel in a variety of ways to suit other purposes. We must rediscover the rich and strange teachings of the gospel—our very own "hokey religion." As Flannery O'Connor is believed to have said about the gospel, "you shall know the truth and the truth will make you odd." As the Apostle Paul wrote in Philippians 3:10, "I want to know Christ and the power of his resurrection and the sharing of his sufferings by becoming like him in his death, if somehow I may attain the resurrection from the dead." Paul's ultimate desire and the shape and content of his message was Christ crucified and resurrected. This, he says in 1 Corinthians, is not what people necessarily want to hear, but it is something which they fundamentally need to hear.

> For Jews demand signs and Greeks demand wisdom, but we proclaim Christ crucified, a stumbling block to the Jews and foolishness to the Gentiles, but to those who are called, both Jews and Greeks, Christ the power of God and the wisdom of God. For God's foolishness is wiser

---

1. Han Solo made a famous quip about the force in *A New Hope*, calling it a "hokey religion," which he clearly did not believe in at that point. I will use this to mean weird or strange, and not make-believe.

than human wisdom, and God's weakness is stronger
than human strength.[2]

Paul's verbal and written proclamation of the gospel is simple: repent or turn fully around and go in a new direction (*metanoia*)
and believe in the life, death, resurrection, and ascension of Jesus
Christ, and live in obedience to his teachings. Paul taught that people were to believe in the message of the gospel in their heads and
hearts, and then were to live it out with their bodies—they were to
have active faith, as the writer of the Epistle of James wrote. Such
faith took on the practical shape of allegiance or obedience and
not simply mental assent. History reveals that people embraced
the firm and challenging message proclaimed by Paul. The same
was true for Jesus himself, and for John the Baptist before him.
And while the people weren't always faithful, the prophets of Israel
proclaimed a message just as firm and strict—but with unfulfilled
longings for the Messiah. The "success" of the prophets is seen
more in terms of their own faithfulness and less in terms of a huge
number of converts or adherents—they were definitely not social
media influencers! By the time of John the Baptist, Jesus, Paul, and
the early church, it was clear that people would respond favorably
to the true gospel if it was proclaimed with passion and conviction.
Respond they did! The book of Acts details the dynamic growth of
the church throughout the ancient Near East. Thousands at a time
responded in faith to the gospel proclaimed by the apostles on and
following the day of Pentecost.

Lest we start off on the wrong foot, we must recognize the fact
that despite these good results, the number of Christ-followers,
was dwarfed by the number of non-Christ-followers. The church
was not a world superpower and was not on pace to become one.[3]
Instead, the church was focused on faithfulness. This is not to say
that Christ-followers didn't want the entire world to be filled with
the love and grace of God, repenting of old ways, and obedient to

2. 1 Cor 1:22–25.

3. Of course this all changed with the conversion of Constantine in 325
and the subsequent adoption of Christianity as the official state religion of the
Roman Empire. This was discussed in a bit more detail in the previous chapter.

the teachings of Christ and the apostles. They most certainly did! The Christian faith is and has always been an evangelical faith—despite how this term may have been co-opted within contemporary US and the broader Western culture.[4] Rather than gimmicky campaigns to reach the most people as fast as possible, the early church was concerned with their witness—or the living embodiment of the gospel message in the form of their own lives with and for others. Alan Kreider has helpfully described this as "the patient ferment of the early church" in a book with the same name.[5] The gist of Kreider's argument is that the church grew not because of any growth campaign, tactical strategy, or market analysis, but instead through being a slow and steady leavening agent in and for the world. While this analysis is not exciting or flashy, I believe that it is nonetheless true. The numerical trends of the contemporary church in North America need not be a cause for lament or shame. Rather, might they be received as an invitation to renewed faithfulness? Perhaps it is time to stop trying to imitate a fast-food bakery chain, and instead focus on being leaven. In so doing, might we, once again, witness a revolution of global proportions?

If we are going to eschew MTD in favor of the gospel of our Lord Jesus Christ, I would propose that the content of the message

4. Larsen, *Cambridge Companion to Evangelical Theology*. At the beginning of chapter 1, Larsen defines an evangelical person as one who is: "(1.) an orthodox Protestant; (2) who stands in the tradition of the global Christian networks arising from the eighteenth-century revival movements associated with John Wesley and George Whitefield; (3) who has a preeminent place for the Bible in her or his Christian life as the divinely inspired, final authority in matters of faith and practice; (4) who stresses reconciliation with God through the atoning work of Jesus Christ on the cross; (5) and who stresses the work of the Holy Spirit in the life of an individual to bring about conversion and an ongoing life of fellowship with God and service to God and others, including the duty of all believers to participate in the task of proclaiming the gospel to all people."

5. Kreider, *Patient Ferment of the Early Church*. This is one of the most important contemporary books on the issue of faith and evangelism. It is both accessible and profound. I can't recommend it strongly enough. I believe that critically appropriating this text is one of the crucial keys to surviving and thriving as a weird ancient religion in the secular, atheistic, and nihilistic Western world.

we proclaim be focused on Jesus. Christology, or the doctrine of Christ, ought to be our starting point, and the basis for all that we say and do. It is the gospel of Jesus Christ, after all. He was and is the *euangelion* or good news, contrasted with the *euangelion* or good news of Caesar proclaimed by the Roman Empire. The Roman imperial cult actively declared the *euangelion* (gospel or good news) of Caesar, who was understood to be divine. In so doing, they baptized all the corrupt practices of the Roman Empire by bathing them in divine light. The early church, on the contrary, intentionally utilized the exact same language to make very radical claims about the person and work of Christ. In Christ Jesus, the kingdom of God came near and has begun spilling over into our everyday lives. The gospel is nothing short of a radical affirmation of the lordship of Jesus above all other lords, and the identification of his coming kingdom as the true goal and hope for the world. The gospel is an affirmation of resurrection life—a radical faith and hope that Jesus was and is for us and that we are meant for him. The gospel attests to the Christian belief that humans are in need of saving or rescue and that try as we might, we cannot achieve this on our own. Jesus is our savior, he is the one who rescues us, and as such he must be central to our faith.

Interestingly, though, a quick scan of contemporary pop culture reveals the opposite. Pop culture appears to be uncomfortable with Jesus, and typically depicts the church and the Christian faith in general as devoid of Jesus as possible. In almost every pop culture engagement with faith and religion—and especially so-called Judeo-Christian faith—Jesus plays almost no role whatsoever. In the recent NBC TV series *The Good Place* (2016–2020), for example, Jesus plays no role. The show is all about the afterlife, and specifically about how one might attain the "good place" and not the "bad place." As the show develops it becomes abundantly clear how badly the earth, and the afterlife, needs a savior, and yet Jesus is never presented as an option. Why is this? The answers are likely myriad, but simply put I believe that humans have always been prone to put our trust in humanism, or in ourselves. On the contrary, Jesus represents the scandal of particularity. This is a term used for a very long time by theologians to refer to the radically specific subject of the Christian faith: Jesus, and his radically specific claims and teachings. Jesus was a man who lived at a very particular time in a very particular place. He taught that his followers were to love others as they wanted to be loved, that they should love even their enemies, and that they should care for the least of these. He taught that we ought to be truth-tellers, have integrity in our businesses, and be radically faithful to our spouses. He taught that the teachings of Israel were the one true religion, and yet he radically reoriented and redefined those same teachings to be more practical. He routinely made Old Testament teachings and law simultaneously more simple and yet more complex. Most importantly, Jesus, and especially his followers, claimed that he was the Messiah even to the extent that he was the actual Son of God and not just the long-awaited anointed one of Israel. For the church, Jesus is God incarnate or enfleshed. Jesus reveals to us, perfectly, who God is and what God wants from us. He always reveals perfectly what humanity is supposed to be as well. Christians proclaim that Jesus was fully God and fully human, with the two natures not being confused with one another and yet not being diametrically split or opposed to one another. In Jesus, the fullness of God was pleased to dwell with humanity, intimately, without conflict, in a way that reveals the ultimate fittedness of creation to its Creator.

In hopes of proclaiming the true gospel, therefore, the church ought to take a cue from the early church and radically wrestle with the incarnation. The early church did this for roughly 300 years until finally settling on some parameters for its beliefs about Jesus at the Council of Nicea (325) and then Constantinople (381). Afterwards, with the two natures of Jesus firmly established, the church turned to an even more confusing struggle for faith and reason: the Trinity. Specifically, the church sought to reconcile the long-standing belief that God is one with the affirmation that Jesus is God and yet not identical with the Father. By including the Holy Spirit as well, they eventually settled on a doctrine called the Trinity, wherein God is said to be one God in three persons, and not three Gods or one God with three manifestations, modes of being, or masks. No, the term *Trinity* is not found in the Bible—it's Latin after all: *Trinitas*. The doctrine of the Trinity represents the church's best work at the impossible and yet requisite task of describing the indescribable. The Christian God is three in one and one in three, always. Even this brief explanation makes one scratch their head. The doctrine of the Trinity is strange, paradoxical, and even, yes, "hokey." It doesn't get much weirder than this. And yet, since the earliest days of the church, the church has said that the core of our faith is faith in Jesus Christ, whose Spirit draws us toward him, and he, in turn, is said to reconcile us with the Father, so that we can again be in loving, covenantal relationship with God: Father, Son, and Holy Spirit. Orthodox Christian faith is Trinitarian faith, period.

Finally, authentic Christian faith, over and against MTD, is a decidedly embodied faith. Christian faith is moral or ethical in that the beliefs espoused by Christians are intended to be embodied by Christians themselves. In the ecclesial tradition I am a part of, we talk about this in terms of holiness, which is essentially the living out of our faith in and for the world. Holiness is the imitation of Christ, by the power of the Holy Spirit, in this present life, with the hope that others might see and encounter the gospel as well. If we believe that Jesus is Lord, then we will obey his teachings such as truth-telling, love of all, even enemies, and care for the least of these. Similarly, embracing Jesus as Lord entails embracing the teachings of the Old Testament as authoritative and helpful in living holy lives. But living in this way must always fight against the temptation to be about rule-following or legalism. Legalism, or rigid rule-following, was one of Jesus' biggest areas of critique. Jesus didn't want people to simply follow the rules for the sake of checking off boxes on a checklist, but because he wanted them/us to be transformed by the underlying principles, values, and presuppositions for the rules: love. Jesus wanted his followers to be people of radical love.

One of the central ways we see and know this love is in the eucharistic meal. As often as Christians receive the eucharistic elements, they experience the grace and love of Jesus anew. It repeatedly reforms and refashions them into members of the body of Christ, commissioned to be Christ's ambassadors to a broken and hurting world. In the eucharistic liturgy, we proclaim the very mystery of our faith: that Christ has died, Christ has risen, and Christ will come again. As the Apostle Paul said, at the table, "as often as you eat this bread and drink this cup, you proclaim Christ's death until he comes again" (1 Cor 11:26). But the Eucharist or communion is about so much more than proclamation. The sacrament is primarily experiential. It is a physical expression and experience of God's grace that is ultimately transformative. The Eucharist makes the church, as the French Roman Catholic theologian Henri de Lubac once argued. In making us into the church, the Eucharist aids in helping us to live out or embody our faith. In the Eucharist, we are re-membered, according to William Cavanaugh.[6]

At its core, then, Christian faith is faith in Jesus Christ as the God-man who fully reveals the Triune God to us, and who, in turn, invites us into restored relationship with God, others, ourselves, and creation as a whole. Christians belief that the key to all of existence can be found in a first-century Jewish peasant who lived in Palestine. Christians believe that he was the incarnation of God—the fullness of God dwelling in the flesh with and for us! He is Emmanuel—God with us! To be quite specific, Christians believe that Jesus is "God from God, light from light, true God from True God, begotten not made, of one being with the Father, through whom all things were made" to quote from the Nicene Creed. Finally, Christians believe that such faith must be active. As Karl Barth was apt to say, theology and ethics are inseparable for Christians. What we say and believe must necessarily translate into what we do—or else we have no real faith at all. Christology, Trinity, and the practical, ethical embodiment of our faith, these are the three ways that the church can avoid the pitfalls of MTD. We mustn't forget, though, that such teachings as Christology and Trinitarian theology are most definitely weird and "religious." These are not user-friendly doctrines and we shouldn't

6. Cavanaugh, *Being Consumed*.

seek to make them so. Such weird beliefs require embodiment and lots of instruction. These teachings make demands of us, which translate into our moral and ethical duties toward God and others. As Bonhoeffer liked to stress, the call to follow Christ was a call to come and die. You cannot be less user-friendly than this! This is the true gospel, however. We see it best embodied in the sacramental practice of the Eucharist, where Christ's body and blood are offered to us again and again, in the hopes that we might be transformed to live for God and others. And again—talk about weird! Eating Christ's body and drinking his blood?! There's a reason why most megachurches don't celebrate the Eucharist very often. It is impractical for so many, yes, but it is also as weird and non-user-friendly as you can possibly get. Eucharistic faith is the opposite of MTD faith. If the church is to proclaim the real gospel, therefore, it is to Christ, the Trinity, and the embodiment of our faith in eucharistically shaped ways, that we must turn.

In conclusion, I can't help but return to the foil I used in so much of the first half of the book: the sermon illustration of seeds being evangelism. I think I was too hard on this image! The ultimate point that my dear colleague was making was that the gospel has all that it needs to grow, and to do so sustainably. If the metaphor that was being used was ultimately an organic one, then it failed, as I have suggested. But this is not the case. The primary metaphor being used was not organic, but rather was focused on the gospel itself. The gospel, unlike a fruit or vegetable seed, does possess all it needs to grow. God causes the seed to grow, as Paul says in 1 Corinthians 3. For too long, we have forgotten this truth. Yes, we are called to sow seeds, to water, and care for them. But ultimately, God grows the seeds. The gospel is self-sufficient. God chooses to work through us, asking us to proclaim the gospel, but makes it clear that God will do the work thereafter. This does not mean that the more we scatter, the bigger the harvest will be. It also does not free us from the hard work of discipleship after a seed begins to grow. Such teaching does not necessarily result in a large church, but it does result in the church.

The church is guilty of becoming overly obsessed with numbers and metrics of growth, assuming that tactics and strategies will result in numbers and growth. As a result, the church modified its message over time to ensure this message would be relevant and accessible to the largest number of people. The problem is that in doing so, the church lost most of its core message, and peddled something far less captivating and truthful. MTD, the gospel of church growth, has failed the church, ruined our credibility, and ultimately been found wanting. It is time for the church to return to the original texts, to the gospel of our Lord Jesus Christ, of Christ crucified and resurrected. It is time to trust that God will establish the church, and that the powers of evil will not prevail against it. We must recognize, though, that this entails no promise of power, prestige, size, or wealth for Christ-followers. If anything, Jesus' actual message to his followers seems to suggest the opposite.

Chapter 10

SMALL-BATCH FAITH

DURING A RECENT TRIP to Los Angeles, my wife and I drove past a small donut shop that looked interesting. I made a mental note of the store and intended to look it up later. Later on I did that very thing, using the all-inclusive encyclopedia of information that we all turn to: Google. I opened my Google Maps app on my iPhone and typed in Sidecar Doughnuts & Coffee in Santa Monica. Not only did Google provide me with driving directions, but I saw that the business had hundreds of very positive, five-star reviews, their hours, website, and any other information I could possibly want about this little establishment. My wife and I vowed to go the next morning. We told our friends that we were staying with and they said they had heard it was quite good. Sidecar did not disappoint! When we entered, we found the place surprisingly small. We noticed a menu, but that was more of a theoretical listing of what they *might* have. In truth the only donuts they had were the small amount of donuts being hand finished by one of the donuts makers—let's call them artisans—who would place them in a designated place in their display case according to their kind. During our trip into the shop there were probably no more than thirty donuts on display. What they did put out was immediately scooped up by those waiting in the small line, including ourselves. We ended up with a small box of donuts consisting more of what they had than what we necessarily would have chosen from their theoretical menu. That said, each and every donut was absolutely delicious. We probably paid twice as much for one of their donuts as we would have elsewhere, but it was worth every penny. You'd better believe that we went back the next morning and encouraged our friends to go as well!

Sidecar is a small-batch donut shop. Small-batch designates "a type of small-scale production in which goods are made in limited quantities, often by means of traditional or artisanal methods."[1] Sidecar is the opposite of Krispy Kreme (see chapter 5)—or else I should clarify, Sidecar is the opposite of Krispy Kreme in the late 1990s to early 2000s. Sidecar doesn't appear to market in any real way other than a nice clean website and their storefronts.[2] At the time of writing, Sidecar has four locations in Southern California, but has plans for further expansion. Sidecar relies on the quality of their product and word-of-mouth advertising for business. In addition, they appear to be committed to ensuring that their digital presence is up-to-date, helpful, and aesthetically pleasing. This makes sense as the internet is the number one place people go to find information on anything these days. Sidecar's donuts are made by hand, in front of customers, all throughout the day and into the evening. Customers at Sidecar get to watch real people make real donuts, by hand, right in front of them. They can choose to hang out and wait if a particular flavor isn't available yet, or they can try something new from the limited selection. From my limited patronage, it was clear that Sidecar is not as concerned with the quantity of their customers or of donuts sold, as they are with the quality of the donuts made. They seem to be convinced that if their donuts are delicious then they will sell and that, in turn, their happy customers will tell others and will repeatedly come back for more. This is a great business model, but not one that will necessarily satisfy corporate investors. I won't claim to know the ins and outs of Sidecar's business model, but from the outside it appears to be thoroughly sustainable and expandable. They have a good product, made in a more expensive and slow manner—by

1. Lexico.com, s.v. "small-batch."
2. Sidecar website, https://www.sidecardoughnuts.com.

hand—but which in turn allows them to charge more for them. They also sell coffee, which is fairly easy to produce and also profitable. The store I went to was small and clean, allowing them to be in a high-profile area but with as little footprint and overhead as possible. Finally, they clearly pay close attention to their online presence. From my limited experience, Sidecar Doughnuts & Coffee is a terrific example of a small-batch business success.

The commitment to a small-batch business model requires discipline, courage, and conviction. Small-batch businesses could, in theory, make more money in that they provide a limited amount of product to a large, and often growing, audience. Small-batch restaurants such as Sidecar do not want leftovers. They do not want to search for other stores and shelves to place their product on. They aren't focused on a large internet-based delivery model. They aren't interested in constantly expanding their offerings to pander to their guests' wants. They don't build newer, bigger buildings. They do not mass-produce their product and deliver them to their locations. Small-batch businesses are almost never chain stores. Such stores, when there are multiple locations, embrace the notion that each location and each baker will make the handmade donuts slightly differently. Though continuity of product is important, what is more important is the handmade artisanal quality of the product.

I believe the church should learn from small-batch businesses and should embrace small-batch faith. Before exploring this more in the conclusion of this book, let us allow a critical remark. In light of chapter 5, along with other comments made throughout this book, your immediate thought might be, "Learn from a business? Isn't that just allowing consumerism to continue to overrun the church?" Great question! My answer is yes and no. Yes, I have urged a business-based or business-influenced model for the church in suggesting small-batch faith. The type of business, though, is key. Though this belief is unpopular, I do not believe there is any escape from the market or consumerism this side of the eschaton. The market, by definition, is all-encompassing. Humans are consuming creatures by nature, and especially by social construct. Barring large-scale catastrophe, or the return of Christ, this will not end. The market can neither be escaped from, nor can we bypass it.[3] I believe it is best to heed Jesus' advice and strive to be as shrewd as serpents and as innocent as doves in our posture in regard to the market. We cannot escape the market, but we can be more careful and intentional about our consumption and endorsement of market optics and practices. This is true for the church as well. The church cannot escape from the market. This does not mean, though, that it must settle for market strategies and consumer analysis as its modus operandi or mode of operation. Perhaps it is possible for the church to affirm its location vis-à-vis the market and yet strive to reject and even oppose the common assumptions and practices of traditional market economics. If this is possible, I think the pathway might lie in the area of what I am calling small-batch faith.

Taking my cue from my observations of Sidecar Doughnuts & Coffee, I suggest that the church must refocus on the following practices in terms of its "business model"[4] and evangelism:

3. One exception to this may be a hermit or monk. A small monastic community might also be an exception, though the larger the community, the greater the chance of some market and consumer influence.

4. There is an inherent danger in using such language as "business model" and other consumeristic terminology—especially since I am critiquing such an understanding of the church. That said, I believe that that the market is inescapable and that we must learn to live in but not of the marketplace, so to speak. Thus, I think it is worthwhile to consider this niche or current within the overall market that appears to operate for slightly different motives than most businesses. That said, making money is still the goal of small-batch businesses and this simply cannot translate over to the church. Rather, I suggest that the emphasis on excellence, confidence in the quality of the "product," and integrity to mission are all things the church can learn from and which can be, albeit carefully, translated into the life of the church.

"Business Model"

- *Attention to detail*

The church must pay close attention to what it does and why it does it. In doing so, taking great care of property and possessions matters a lot. Small-batch business values quality over quantity. As such, the church can learn from small-batch business about the importance of curating a beautiful and clean space to operate in. This also applies to practices as well. The old adage "if it's worth doing, it's worth doing well" applies.

- *Good maintenance of current buildings and grounds, with little emphasis on new, and especially bigger, buildings*

These are generalized statements of course, and generally speaking, small-batch faith is not so interested in new and bigger buildings, but in clean, organized, and debt-free buildings.

- *Every person matters—individual focus rather than mass-appeal*

The same principle applies to people. People matter. Every person matters. Small-batch business understands that people don't enter because they received mass-mailers, or as a result of a large-scale marketing campaign, but because they likely heard that their product was good, and they had to experience it for themselves.

- *Emphasis on experience—pastors as artisans and curators*

Embracing the term *artisan* or *curator* is a helpful step in the right direction for pastors in this "model." Pastoring truly is an art form, as Eugene Peterson has taught us.

- *Commitment to preaching the true gospel (see chapter 9) in easy-to-understand, and yet non-user-friendly ways*

This is key. The "product," to borrow from the consumer business model, is what drives this model. If the church presents the gospel clearly and unashamedly, it will take root and grow. This will likely not happen with the sort of numbers the church has grown accustomed to, but the chances are much greater that the roots of faith will go down deeper and take hold.

- *Commitment to clean and up-to-date digital presence*

Small-batch business teaches us that we do not have to concern ourselves with the latest and greatest market research and analysis. The church does not need to pursue a complicated marketing strategy, and it certainly does not need to employ a social media influencer! However, the church must ensure that its website is up to date, cleanly organized, and easy to follow.

- *Overall focus on sustainability*

In everything the church does, it should proceed with fixed attention upon sustainability. This includes, but greatly surpasses, our environmental footprint. One of the reasons the church is in the mess it is in today is because it failed to consider the sustainability or lack thereof of its various practices.

Evangelism

- *Hospitality*

Small-batch businesses typically stress outstanding hospitality to their customers. They are concerned with curating a wonderful experience for their patrons in hopes that they will come back and tell others. Many such businesses also seem to value the type of community created by such hospitality, as if such hospitality will slowly help improve their community and world. The church shares this with such businesses. We are called to be beacons of hospitality in a mostly inhospitable world. The church is certainly called to serve those who come in, but we are equally called to serve those outside. This is something that makes the church unique and even strange. In fact, most historians and sociologists of religion point to Christian hospitality to strangers and even enemies as one of the key factors in the explosive growth of the early church. In this way, hospitality is central to both our "business model" and also to evangelism.

- *The audience is not those outside with no interest in our "product," but those that want to come in*

Small-batch business reminds us that our "product" is what is most important. Our "product"—the gospel—will grow, take root, and be embraced with minimal work on our part. This cannot happen, though, unless we preach the real gospel, as discussed in chapter 9. In order to stay true to this, the church should focus less on attracting outsiders, and more on teaching, equipping, and discipling those who do respond and who want to learn more about the gospel.

- *Rejection of marketing or attractional events*

This point has been championed by so many in recent years that it does not need much explanation. Attractional events almost never pan out in terms of producing new converts. What's more, even if they do succeed in attracting new members/attenders, the overwhelming odds are that such new members/attenders are not new to faith, but are simply recycled Christians out church shopping. In order to keep these new members/attenders engaged the church will have to continue to offer bigger, better, and more expensive attractional events.

- *Embrace of outward-focused, service-oriented events*

Contrary to the previous point, small-batch business teach us that people are looking for opportunities to serve and give back to their local and global communities. The success of one-for-one business models such as Tom's Shoes, businesses that strive to reduce their social and environmental impact, and the success of fair-trade products in general, are all good examples of this principle. Small-batch faith embraces service and environmental and social stewardship as its marketing or evangelism.

- *Reliance upon word-of-mouth marketing*

Finally, small-batch business relies almost exclusively, and often with great results, upon the quality of its products, and the positive experiences of its consumers. Small-batch businesses do not usually seek to meet a consumeristic need so much as to offer a product that they believe is good. They believe that if the product is good, people will desire it. So too, the church should trust in the quality of its product, vis-à-vis the gospel, and focus what it can on the curation of a positive experience for its guests.

Let there be no confusion: the church is not a business, the gospel is not a product, and people are not (simply) consumers. What I am urging is not simply another business or marketing strategy for the church. And yet, I believe there is much we can learn from this small niche within the marketplace. Like small-batch businesses, commitment to such practices within the current market environment will require the church to possess discipline, courage, and conviction, and above all else, faithfulness. The embrace of small-batch faith will likely translate into a future with fewer full-time, paid, professional clergy, and more bi-vocational, tent-making pastors. Denominational structures will likely be affected, as well, as less time and energy are spent focusing on outdated models of ecclesial institutionalism. In short, this will likely mean a drastic change for clergy.[5] The need for such changes is something I have observed in every one of my senior or lead pastor assignments. It is beyond the scope of this book to explore the reality and ramifications of these possibilities. Suffice it to say, I believe the church is up to the task. As the church dies, it is actually

5. This is diagnosis and not advocacy. I am not critiquing the institutional church so much as helping identify a way forward in light of the slow death identified in part 1 of this book. I have served as a full-time pastor for over ten years. I am a proud member of a denomination that would likely struggle in the scenario I am describing. Institutionalism will not help us in this scenario, though. Rather, I think such dogged commitment to maintaining the apparatus of our institutions will prevent resurrection and new life from occurring. We have to be open to the likelihood that the church will need to change significantly if it is to survive and even thrive in the future.

being reborn—refashioned into a resurrection community, filled full with the grace of God. The church will not die—it cannot die! We must not confuse the particularly contemporary structure and model, though, with its ultimate purpose and calling. Nowhere in the New Testament does it say that the church must be a large institution characterized by extensive bureaucracy and staffed by a large number of (clergy or non-clergy) business managers. While these positions may seem quite necessary today, one cannot help but wonder if such bureaucracy is beginning to hinder the church from moving into the creative future that lies ahead. By carefully taking cues from small-batch business community, the church just might be able to adapt and thrive in the changing climate of secularism and anti-Christianity.

Chapter 11

THE FUTURE OF THE CHURCH IN NORTH AMERICA

Toward a New Beginning

> For there is hope for a tree, if it is cut down, that it will sprout again, and that its shoots will not cease. Though its root grows old in the earth, and its stump dies in the ground, yet at the scent of water it will bud and put forth branches like a young plant.
> —Job 14:7–9

FROM MANY VANTAGE POINTS, the picture I have painted in this short book is admittedly bleak. The church in North America is certainly on the decline. Attendance in most places is plummeting. The age of average attenders is steadily rising, with fewer and fewer young people engaging in any real way. Statistics suggest that most young people are leaving and rather than remaining open to the church at a later date via a posture of agnosticism, they are instead turning toward a posture of atheism. This group is best described as the "Nones" or people of no faith, or even "Uns," people of anti-faith. This latter group, characterized by antagonism toward the church, is growing at an alarmingly rapid pace. In other words, we are not simply observing people leaving the church, we are witnessing people turn against the church in a posture of open defiance and even hostility. The church is increasingly believed to be outdated, racist, homophobic, and unwilling to change. In light of these observations, questions and conversations about its possible death are certainly appropriate. What will the church look like in the future? Will it have a future? If so—and I strongly suggest that it will—what will that future look like?

In this final chapter I intend to suggest a few possibilities for what we need to consider as we move toward the future of the church in North America. I believe the church certainly does have a future. I believe that future to be one that is full of hope and possibility. I believe, though, that the future will be incredibly different than the reality that we have taken for granted in the Western world for the last several hundred years—possibly even for our entire existence after Constantine's conversion in 325. I believe this future is truly exciting, for it offers us a chance to start over, to disentangle ourselves from some really bad practices and positions, and return to our first love: the gospel of our Lord and Savior Jesus Christ. In a word, the way forward is the path of resurrection. We are resurrection people, after all. As Paul declares in 1 Corinthians 15, if there is no resurrection then we are to be pitied and our faith and our proclamation—in other words our very lives—have been lived in vain. Everything about the Christian faith is rubbish if there is no resurrection. But of course for Paul there is resurrection—both Christ's and our own! We who are baptized, according to Paul's teachings, have been crucified with Christ and have been raised anew with him in resurrection life. We live our lives, then, at the intersection of the old and the new, experiencing the ways of sin and death and yet glimpsing and experiencing resurrection. Through the ongoing work of the Holy Spirit, we are made capable of living into the resurrection as holy people here and now, for the sake of the world.[1] This gospel is truly transformational, as it

---

1. N. T. Wright's *Surprised by Hope* provides a terrific explanation of the central role that resurrection is to play in the lives of Christians and in our proclamation of the gospel.

brings life to decay and death. We experience this in our lives and we are to bring this transformation to those around us by sharing the gospel with them in word and deed. Our lives, in other words, are to become tiny beacons of resurrection life amid darkness, destruction, doubt, and death.

What we fail to realize, though, is that for most, what I've described as darkness, destruction, doubt, and death is simply the given that they operate within. Like the prisoners in Plato's cave, they take what they see at face value and assume there are no options. But of course, we know there are options. There is a different way. Light exists beyond and outside the darkness. For the church to witness to this different reality, though, it must be bold, clear, and confident of its message. Once again, as Stanley Hauerwas declared several decades ago, the most important thing for the church is to be the church.[2] What Hauerwas means is that for the world to know it is, in fact, the world, the church must embrace its own identity—strange as it may be! This thesis is even more important today than it was when Hauerwas first wrote it. We must spend more time on the things that make us unique—the things we don't have in common with others. We must knowingly and proudly pick up the mantle of our "hokey religion" and embrace our religious beliefs and practices as central to who we are as people. Make no mistake, though, this is no isolationist decree. This should also not be received as an encouragement to neglect social justice and equality, by limiting our focus to the spiritual life. As has already been argued in this book, chapter 9 in particular, our faith is necessarily practical and ethical. The Christian faith is an embodied or lived out faith. What we believe is meant to inform how we live. Thus, as we embrace our strange religious beliefs—beliefs that necessarily distance us from others—we are continually reminded of our need for others and our call to serve them. In the end, then, Christians must simultaneously become distant from others due to our unique beliefs, and yet are more closely drawn to others due to the practices that our beliefs inspire and require.

2. Hauerwas, "Reforming Christian Social Ethics."

This is no easy task. Embracing our peculiar beliefs and practices creates distance between ourselves and those that we may know and love. Furthermore that distance is often filled up with awkwardness, tension, and even rejection based on the perception that we are no longer "one of them." As we travel further on the journey of discipleship, we become less and less intelligible to those that we used to be close to. In some situations, this distance even becomes filled with violence, as Christians are persecuted physically for their faith. Do not misunderstand: following Christ leads to death. This is true personally, and I think it is also true for the church. The gospel is not convenient, popular, or even fun. It can be those things, but it often is not. It is, however, true. Truth, it is said, sets one free. That freedom, however, comes with a price. The price it cost Jesus was death. We are foolish if we think it does not require death (in one way or another) of us as well. In this book I have suggested that the church is, in a way, dying. I believe the institutional church, as we have know it for a very long time, is dying. This is no simple thing, however. It is not enough to say that the church is dying or is dead—we are not materialists after all. We believe there is more than death. Death is not the end but the end of the beginning. Why should this not be true for the church as well? Is the church not the foretaste of the kingdom of God, about which we proudly affirm that it will have no end? Does the church not participate in the already-but-not-yet kingdom of God? Is the church not a signpost on the way of discipleship? So what if the church goes the way of the saints, and even of her Lord? What is death, anyway, especially given our belief in resurrection? To say that the church is dying, therefore, is not a sentence that can end in a period or full stop. Instead, this sentence must always be followed by a comma, for it is but a dependent clause in a much larger sentence. That sentence goes something like this: the church is dying, but its death is the death of discipleship required of us all. It will be, and is already being, reborn into new and unending life in him. For the Christian, death is a necessary part of resurrection. The same is true for the church. Death and resurrection are inseparable in the Christian faith. We are encouraged not to be afraid of death. As a pastor, I am to assist people in grieving, allow them to do so, but also to encourage them with the gospel to remember that we do not believe that this is the end. As a pastor I am charged with preaching resurrection. Perhaps it is time for the church to go through this process itself. As we move through death into resurrection, I would like to suggest four key things to keep in mind.

First, it is important to understand and accept that much of our "soil," so to speak, in North America and most of the West, has been poisoned by our own poor and excessive cultivation. We have abused the ground, and even poisoned it to the point that we cannot expect it to bear fruit as it used to. And remember, much of the "fruit" that was borne previously was not the fruit of the real Christian faith but of something else, a perversion of the Christian faith. There is not much we can do about this. The best way to allow soil to heal is to let it be for a number of years. Right off the bat, then, we must embrace a future that does not involve massive "harvests." The future of the church, therefore, looks more like an urban raised-bed garden than a commercial farm. Cultivating a raised-bed garden requires a prioritization of one's limited space, purchasing and mixing the right types of soils, and then tending it like any farmer would tend her crops. Each year the soil must be carefully reexamined, and compost and other nutrients must be added, if it is to bear fruit. This has always been my challenge with raised-bed gardening. I have never taken the time to recultivate the soil after the first year, and I've noticed that each subsequent harvest is smaller and smaller. I routinely made the mistake of thinking that the soil was neutral and forgot how large a role it plays in the growing of the crop. Pastoral ministry in the age to come will need to learn from such failures and carefully tend the soil. While letting the larger fields go fallow, we must carefully tend to the small beds that we are farming, in order to continue to reap a harvest.

In other words, we can no longer assume that if we scatter the seed, we will reap a harvest. The soil is simply unwilling to bring forth a crop the size of our expectations. And again, if we are honest, it probably never did bring forth such a harvest of true faith. This means that the future we are moving toward, as a church, is likely to be a future characterized by small churches. Just as in the analogy, the likely future for the church in North America looks much more like a prolific urban raised-bed garden and not like a commercial farm. Harvest will come, and it will be widespread, but there will be lots of small harvests. Our future is one of raised-bed heirloom tomatoes and not GMO mass-produced tomatoes. To continue the metaphor, this means our future will taste better, look and feel more interesting, but also be much smaller and more unique. In this way the future of the church in North America is appealing and interesting and delicious! What has gone unsaid up to this point, though, is that such small gardens cannot sustain the sort of infrastructure the church has grown to assume as normal. Large buildings, denominational headquarters, paid overseers, large pastoral staff with specialized ministry focuses, and even full-time paid pastors can no longer be the assumption. Urban raised-bed gardens simply cannot sustain whole restaurants or grocery stores, and certainly not restaurant or grocery store chains. This point is scary for many pastors and religious professionals like myself, but that does not make it any less true. The writing is on the wall. The question is how we will receive it. Will we cower or pretend we do not see it, or will we embrace this new reality as faithful entrepreneurs and innovators? My hope is that we can go the way of the latter. Jobs can be lost, security can be forfeited, but our faith must endure. As clergy, we were not called to a full-time job with a pension and benefits, but to serve God by serving God's people and by teaching and preaching the gospel. For most of the history of the church, and in much of the world today, pastors are not paid enough to live on, and certainly don't receive either a pension or benefits. I do not look forward to this change, but I know it is coming. The negatives are clear. The positives, though, remain to be seen. It might be that such changes will help lessen the distinction between priesthood and laity and result in an increase in ownership and service by non-pastoral leaders. The result, in other words, might be the opening up of leadership and power, resulting in a more communal existence. This is surely a good thing.

Second, it is absolutely essential for the church to disentangle itself from partisan politics. The church should seek justice, but it should not seek power. The church does not need to work to become more and more established. The more and more established or stable one becomes usually results in laziness anyway! No, the church must move toward a posture of radical service to the other—particularly the marginalized and oppressed—through its own local expressions of embodied or active faith, rather than believing that it is the job of a government to do such work. We should assume that governments—all of them—will always be skeptical of us at best or opposed to us at worst, given the fact that we declare that someone else is Lord and Savior. The church, in other words, should seek to be agents of local social reform, trusting that others will do the same in all other communities and that together we will exist as transformative agents in our world, as we wait for the coming reign of our God and King, whose kingdom is perfectly just, and which will have no end.

This is true for the "religious or Christian Left" as much as it is for the "Christian right." Both exist, at the end of the day, as two sides of the same coin. Their confused loyalty places ultimate allegiance in human reason, the party, the state, a document such as a constitution, or some other equally well-intended but flawed and temporary thing. Neither right nor left is exempt from this. Partisan politics—especially civil religion—has played a significant role in the death of the church. The way of resurrection is the way of *the* King and Savior. The church is not called to serve as a chaplain to the state. Nowhere does Jesus encourage such engagement. The church ought to learn from the ancient letters from Pliny to Roman Emperor Trajan in which Pliny notes the strangeness of Christians for being the most wonderful citizens imaginable except that they refused to participate in the Caesar pledge. In ancient pre-Constantinian Rome, Christians thought of themselves as resident aliens or strangers in Rome. They sought neither persecution nor political power. They fell in line, served others, and didn't seek attention. They did their duty when at all possible, except when asked to worship anyone or thing other than Jesus. Jesus was Lord, and no other. They appear to have been mostly disinterested in national or global politics, and they certainly didn't pursue power, but they most certainly did work toward the betterment of their individual communities. In this way the early Christians were thoroughly political without beings servants of, or chaplains to, the state.

People are fed up with witnessing the church embrace certain elected officials as if they are the savior of the church. This is especially true of those with incredibly sketchy personal lives and histories. Such endorsements are problematic at best and heretical at worst. The people of the world have seen. They've taken note. They are repulsed by our unfaithful and hypocritical support of such clearly flawed political candidates. Enough is enough. Let us return to our first love, and serve Jesus alone as our Lord and Savior, working for justice and reform in our local communities.

Third, I suggest that the way forward for the church in North America is to unashamedly proclaim the gospel, paying particular attention to the doctrines of Christology and Trinity with a decidedly practical and ethical focus. We simply must learn from the failures fo the last few centuries and realize that the message we preach has a direct connection to the types of converts we will see. If we proclaim a message of health, wealth, and prosperity, then we will receive those looking for health, wealth, and prosperity into the church. Then, when sickness and/or financial difficulties happen to these individuals, their faith will be shaken and they will leave the church. Similarly, if the message we proclaim is designed for maximum accessibility—something like moral therapeutic deism—then converts will be converted to this same shallow and bland faith. They will be cheerful agnostics, believing that there is a God who wants them to be happy, even the best versions of themselves. They'll go to church and seek personal satisfaction. Then, when they struggle, or when they see that others, such as therapists, twelve-step programs, CrossFit groups, MOPS, and so many others might offer the same or better personal support in smaller, more intimate settings, they will leave and seek personal support and growth in those places. The message we preach will directly impact the type of conversions we see. If we proclaim anything other than the Jesus of the gospel—Christ crucified and resurrected—then we will, similarly, convert people to something or someone other than the Jesus of the gospel.

The Jesus of the gospel cares deeply for all. He is a friend of sinners. He is a help to those in need. He cares deeply for the alien, orphan, and widow as the Old Testament instructed the people of Israel. The Jesus of the gospel also seems unwilling to write off the rich and powerful, frequently engaging with them in conversation and dining with them. He seems to care equally about rich and poor, women and men; every type of social distinction one might like to add falls within Jesus's love and concern. There is no reason to try to dumb down this Jesus, therefore, or make him more appealing. The church exists today because Jesus is appealing—he is the Father's appeal after all, sent to the world in the attempt at ultimate reconciliation. God does not need our help making Jesus more accessible to people. God does need our help, though, in sharing this Jesus, as witnessed to in Scripture, through the lens of our own personal experiences and believes. We are called to be witnesses, not interpreters. We are called to tell the story of Jesus, and not try to make the story of Jesus more believable, more accessible, or more anything! Jesus is enough. What's more, Jesus promises that the Holy Spirit will give us words to say in such situations and that the Holy Spirit is already at work in the lives of those that are far away from God, cultivating the soil of their lives for the reception and growth of the gospel. We do not need to change the message for better results—we just need to proclaim the message.

We must proclaim the gospel, therefore, and specifically the story of Jesus Christ crucified and resurrected. The church has long affirmed this basic outline, taken from the Apostle's Creed, of the story of Jesus that is the main content of the gospel:

> We believe in Jesus Christ, his (the Father's) only Son, our Lord.
> He was conceived by the power of the Holy Spirit and born of the Virgin Mary. He suffered under Pontus

Pilate, was crucified, died, and was buried. He descended
to the dead. On the third day he rose again.
He ascended into heaven, and is seated at the right hand
of the Father.
He will come again to judge the living and the dead.

We should further clarify the content of our message with this
statement from the Nicene Creed:

We believe in one Lord, Jesus Christ, the only Son of
God, eternally begotten of the Father, God from God,
Light from Light, true God from true God, begotten,
not made, of one Being with the Father. Through him all
things were made.
For us and for our salvation he came down from heaven:
By the power of the Holy Spirit he became incarnate
from the Virgin Mary and was made man.
For our sake he was crucified under Pontus Pilate; he suf-
fered death and was buried.
On the third day he rose again in accordance with the
Scriptures; he ascended into heaven and is seated at the
right hand of the Father.
He will come again in glory to judge the living and the
dead, and his kingdom will have no end.

This is to be the basic content of our message. In summary, this
message consists of the following key points:

- The incarnation of the Son via the virgin birth by the power
  of the Holy Spirit

- Jesus, the only Son of the Father, is one with the Father

- Jesus was crucified under Pontus Pilate—dead and buried

- Jesus' resurrection occurred on the third day

- Jesus ascended to heaven, where he waits until an unknown
  time when he will return, bringing judgment and heaven itself with him

- The kingdom Jesus brings will have no end

These beliefs are peculiar, strange, specific, and all beyond
the limits of logical proof. These are claims that must be believed,

beyond and apart from known evidence, personal experience, or modern scientific evidence. If these are not the sort of strange and even "hokey" beliefs that constitute a religion, I do not know what they are. These beliefs cannot be proven, but they are compelling. It is enough to proclaim them, share why one believes them, and then live out the truth of these beliefs with and for others. This is the life of the Christian, and it is this that the church must return to. The church is, at its core, a group of people connected by their peculiar beliefs, who at once are both distinct from those around them, and yet bound to serve and care of those around them regardless of their own opinions, beliefs, and/or practices. This is Christian witness. We need not water down the gospel in order to serve others. Service is enough. We serve because we believe. People will ask why we do what we do. When this happens, the gospel can be shared. When the gospel is shared, it should be shared from a posture of humility mixed with boldness and faith. "Yeah, I know this is weird, but this is what I believe. This has been my experience of faith. This is why I am part of the church. This is why I do what I do. If you want to know more, come and see." This is how a basic evangelistic conversation ought to go. Notice that such a conversation begins when the Christian is asked about their faith. Once asked, she is free to share a summary of the gospel of Jesus Christ. She acknowledges that much of this might seem strange, but that she believes it nonetheless. Then she invites the other to come and see—come and experience. In this way, the gospel maintains its integrity. The friend, relative, or neighbor who asks is made aware of the basic peculiarities of the Christian faith and is invited to come and see or experience this for themselves. "Come and try it out," in other words. For the church, this means that we ought to assume that most visitors, when the come, are coming because they want to know what the church is all about. They do not want to be the recipients of a performance intended to make them believe at all costs, one that sacrifices the truth of the gospel for intelligibility. This is likely not what brought them in the first place. Rather, they want to learn what it is that Christians actually believe. They want to experience the mystery and grace of true

Eucharist. They want to encounter the God of the Christian faith, they want to experience Jesus for themselves. They are prepared for weirdness. We should not be afraid, therefore, to display the weirdness of our faith. In this way, they will know exactly what they are signing up for, so to speak.

Such evangelism will most assuredly result in fewer converts. I cannot help but think, though, that those who do throw their lot in with the church in its attempt to obediently follow the Lamb that was slain from the foundations of the world, will be more likely to stick with it when their lives grow challenging, when they experience pain, suffering, and death, or when they wrestle with doubt. Such faith will, hopefully, have the sort of staying power and depth necessary to endure such common and extremely difficult situations.

Finally, as the church moves through death into resurrection, I believe it must be willing to "do" church very differently. If the future of the church is to be a future characterized by much smaller numbers, less denominational infrastructure, fewer large buildings—indeed fewer designated church buildings at all, and fewer paid clergy—then the future of the church will look differently by necessity. This is not necessarily a bad thing. This future seems quite similar to the reality of the early church, in fact. Designated buildings, paid clergy, and denominational infrastructure are not necessary after all. These things are nice, and arguably make us more comfortable, but they are not essential. Essential to the ability to be the church is the ability to gather, read Scripture, pray, participate in the Eucharist, and then live out the gospel in public.[3] At their core, none of these things requires much money,

3. This book was completed during the coronavirus pandemic of 2020. During this time, the ability of the church to gather was sorely tested. The church did its best to continue worshiping through digital media such as Zoom, Facebook Live, live-streaming, and so forth. We also were constantly reminded that the church was not closed, despite not physically gathering. Such statements were true and helpful and I appreciate the encouragement. That said, one of the most important things that the church does is to physically gather together. Christian sociologists have long affirmed this to be a fundamental truth of Christian worship—that gathering together is one of the most important things that we do, and they have encouraged us to not

paid clergy, or a (large) building set aside solely for church use. Again, these things are all nice and make things more comfortable, but they are not essential. As I suggested in chapter 10, I think that the church ought to take a cue from small-batch businesses as it reenvisions itself for the future. Such churches might consider blurring the lines between worship and service, so that the two become intimately connected. Perhaps in the secular, and un- or anti-Christian Western world, churches should embrace a peculiar communal service as an extension of their faith and practice. As such, churches become a welcome and vital part of each local community, they receive modest income to help support clergy, worship needs, and communal charity. Such churches are more missional outposts than traditional churches as most of us have come to know them. The following is a non-exhaustive list of ideas for what such churches might look like:

- A coffee shop focused on selling fair-trade, single-origin cof-fees and teas, locally made pastries, and providing communal space for people to share life. The pastor or pastoral staff works at, and even manages, the shop, as a way of supporting themselves and the ministry. Out of this entrepreneurial en-deavor, a small church is formed. This church does not need financial support and it does not need to pay a pastor or staff, because the model itself is self-sustaining.

---

overlook this simple fact. Christian worship is not a solitary, passive experience. In worship, we are gathered together and physically knit together into the very body of Christ before being sent out into the world to be the hands and feet of God. The church is routinely gathered, scattered, and gathered back in. As my good friend Brent Peterson likes to say, we are repeatedly breathed in, breathed out, and then breathed back in by the Holy Spirit in Christian worship. And so, while I conducted digital meetings like everyone else, I also mourned the lack of physical presence. And I suggest that we not mistake the legal and ethical mandate to socially or physically distance from one another as a recommended way of worshiping moving forward. The Christian faith is a communal faith. It is an embodied faith. It is a physical faith. If and when the world experiences such a phenomenon again, we will need to balance the need for safety and security with the blatant truth that we are physical and social creatures, and that our worship is physical, communal, and social in nature.

- A bike repair shop (or similar small business) that is owned and operated by a pastor/missionary in an urban sector whose goal is to offer superb customer service for those needing bike repair, reduce the environmental footprint of those in the community, and the intentional employment of urban youth, men and women in recovery. These people often have little to no job experience and need to learn good work skills along with earning a paycheck. All the while, this small business is able to also serve as a meeting space for a fledgling church plant and/or small group that has no need of financially supporting a pastor or building.

- A rural youth engagement center aimed at providing mentoring, counseling, friendship, and space for youth to come together in positive, life-giving ways. Such a center might be funded and staffed through an ecumenical effort of many local churches, none of which could afford to hire a youth pastor on their own, but instead, pool together modest resources to provide a space and a person or team to minister to all youth in a given area beyond the walls of a particular church.

- A traditional church that transitions into placing its successful food-bank ministry into its primary identity in the community by aligning worship services with volunteering. Members and attenders gather on a Saturday or Sunday to make ready the goods and/or the meal that will be provided to the public. Once ready, they pause and spend an hour worshiping together, inviting the public to join them if they are interested, before opening the food and clothing distribution to the public. Or perhaps they hold a worship service immediately following clean-up, again inviting those they have served to join them if they are interested. In this way, the traditional church has made itself invaluable to the community, reduced the commitment level of is members by consolidating meeting times to one day, and aligned its message with its practices. Such a church can say, "What we believe is what we do." Such a church may still rely on tithes and offerings to support itself, but it has succeeded in merging mission with worship. This church no longer has to persuade people to serve because to worship at this church is to serve and to serve is to worship. In this way, the church's model has more readily been brought into alignment with the gospel. I cannot help but think that this will result in the alignment of the its members with the gospel as well.

There is truly no end to the possibilities for such creative instantiations of the church. Such creative expressions of church can be for-profit or nonprofit businesses. Some will not be businesses at all. Common to most of these creative church options is the assumption that clergy will need to be tent-makers, or bi-vocational. Sustainability will be key for these creative ministers. Some will find that merging together a business such as a coffee shop, restaurant, thrift store, bookstore, counseling center or the like with their church will be best. For others, a job elsewhere in the secular world that provides for their family financially, will allow them to plant a church in their home, or will provide them with the funds necessary to procure a space. Such churches will then, hopefully, begin to pool resources together in order to ensure that the pastor does not have to continue to pay for the meeting space, utilities, and other expenses. Every one of these creative instantiations of the church will be different because every community and every pastor is different. Creativity and a spirit of entrepreneurship will be essential. I suggest that small-batch businesses like Sidecar Doughnuts in Los Angeles, or the network of Blend Coffee Shops in Scotland,[4] serve as examples for the church in discerning creative entrepreneurial options for the future.

4. Blend is a network of for-profit coffee shops in Scotland owned and operated by Christian friends Alan, Derrick, Gregor, and Sundeep with the purpose of providing excellent coffee, building community, and planting churches in Scotland. They have been very successful with all of these things. I believe that much of their success lies in the fact that they are for-profit businesses, aimed at providing a truly excellent product and experience. This has not been sacrificed for the goal of planting a church or church-type community. As a result, Blend has been recognized as an outstanding business and part of the community and it has also succeeded at attracting non-Christians from the

Such churches must be creative. They must believe in their message or "product," that is, the gospel. They must not pander to the public, believing that they need to impress, water down, or create a false need for what they have to offer. Instead, such churches must exegete their communities, discover the needs that are there, discern what business options might be present that would allow for sustainable ministry to begin and flourish, and then they must serve their community with honesty and integrity. As they do so, community members, neighbors, patrons, and others will begin to take notice and ask questions. They might respond to opportunities to gather for a Bible study, a book study, a film group, to farm an urban raised-bed garden space, or some other opportunity offered by the church. In short, in the future I'm describing, the church in North America, and other places in the radically secularized Western world, will merge worship with service to the community. Such churches will often lead with service, but offer the opportunity to for worship. And as we have seen, such opportunities for worship will assume that people understand that they are in for something that is strange, other, mysterious, and, well, religious! The church will blend passionate service to its community with unapologetically robust teaching about its crucified and risen Lord, the Triune God, and all the while explain the need to put faith into action.

This future I'm describing is unquestionably different from the reality that most of us have known. It is unknown and it can seem scary. The implications are vast and challenging for denominations, for existing churches—especially those with large buildings that are not paid for yet, and for clergy. I will not pretend to have all the answers and I will not pretend that any of this is easy. I do firmly believe, however, that less infrastructure and professional

community and creating small church communities out of their coffee shop connections. Currently operating in Perth, Paisley (Glasgow area), Dundee, and likely soon in Edinburgh, Blend is a phenomenal example of the sort of community I am describing and prescribing as a valid expression of the church in the secular Western world in which we live. For more information on Blend, visit their website at http://blendcoffee.co.uk. If you visit, be sure to tell them that Rusty sent you—maybe they will give you a free coffee.

support is not the same as failure, and that the death of the church as we know it is not truly death, but rather an invitation into the creative, restorative, regenerative resurrection life offered by our Savior. The future will be different, yes. We will walk through darkness to get there. But after the darkness of the night and of death, comes the unimaginably splendid rising of the Son, and with that new life—resurrection.

BIBLIOGRAPHY

Athanasius. *On the Incarnation*. York, UK: Empire, 2012.

Bethke, Jefferson. "Why I Hate Religion, But Love Jesus." YouTube video, 4:03. January 10, 2012. https://youtu.be/1IAhDGYlpqY.

Brian, Rustin. "Beyond Syncretism: On the Competing Liturgies of North American Civil Religion and the Church." In *In Spirit and in Truth: Philosophical Reflections on Liturgy and Worship*, edited by Wm. Curtis Holtzen and Matthew Hill, 165–80. Claremont Studies in Methodism & Wesleyanism 1. Claremont, CA: Claremont University Press, 2016.

Cavanaugh, William. *Being Consumed: Economics and Christian Desire*. Grand Rapids: Eerdmans, 2008.

———. *The Myth of Religious Violence*. Oxford: Oxford University Press, 2009.

Dean, Kendra Creasy. *The Almost Christian: What the Faith of Our Teenagers Is Telling the American Church*. New York: Oxford University Press, 2010.

"Falwell Dismisses Photo of Him and Trump and *Playboy* Magazine." *New York Post*, June 22, 2016. https://nypost.com/2016/06/22/falwell-dismisses-photo-of-him-trump-and-playboy-mag/.

Gaiman, Neil. *The Annotated American Gods*. New York: William and Morrow, 2020.

Gallup. "Church Membership Down Sharply in the Past Two Decades." https://news.gallup.com/poll/248837/church-membership-down-sharply-past-two-decades.aspx.

Graham, David A., and Elaine Godfrey. "If These Allegations Are True, He Must Step Aside." *Atlantic*, November 2017. https://www.theatlantic.com/politics/archive/2017/11/roy-moore/545471/.

Gutierrez, Gustavo. *A Theology of Liberation*. Maryknoll, NY: Orbis, 1988.

Gunton, Colin. *The Actuality of Atonement: A Study of Metaphor, Rationality, and the Christian Tradition*. Grand Rapids: Eerdmans, 1989.

Hauerwas, Stanley. "Reforming Christian Social Ethics: Ten Theses." In *The Hauerwas Reader*, edited by John Berkman and Michael Cartwright, 111–15. Durham, NC: Duke University Press, 2001.

Hugo, Victor. *Les Misérables*. New York: Modern Library, 2008.

Johnson, Rian, dir. *Star Wars: The Last Jedi*. Los Angeles: Disney, 2017.

Jones, Jeffrey M. "U.S. Church Membership Down Sharply in Past Two Decades." *Gallup*, April 18, 2019. https://news.gallup.com/poll/248837/church-membership-down-sharply-past-two-decades.aspx.

Joyce, James. *Ulysses*. Oxford: Oxford University Press, 2008.

Kowitt, Beth. "Behind the Krispy Kreme Turnaround." *Fortune*, June 27, 2013. https://fortune.com/2013/06/27/behind-the-krispy-kreme-turnaround/.

Kreider, Alan. *The Patient Ferment of the Early Church: The Improbable Rise of Christianity in the Roman Empire*. Grand Rapids: Baker Academic, 2016.

Larsen, Timothy. *The Cambridge Companion to Evangelical Theology*. Cambridge: Cambridge University Press, 2007.

MacIntyre, Alasdair. *After Virtue*. 3rd ed. Notre Dame, IN: University of Notre Dame Press, 2007.

Martínez, Jessica. "How the Faithful Voted: A Preliminary 2016 Analysis." Pew Research Center, November 9, 2016. https://www.pewresearch.org/fact-tank/2016/11/09/how-the-faithful-voted-a-preliminary-2016-analysis/.

Marx, Karl. *A Contribution to the Critique of Hegel's Philosophy of Right*. Cambridge: Cambridge University Press, 1977.

McCarthy, Niall. "America's Most & Least Trusted Professions." *Forbes*, January 11, 2019. https://www.forbes.com/sites/niallmccarthy/2019/01/11/americas-most-least-trusted-professions-infographic/#42a58f5a7e94.

Nietzsche, Friedrich. *Beyond Good and Evil: Prelude to a Philosophy of the Future*. New York: Vintage, 1989.

Pew Research Center. "America's Changing Religious Landscape." Pew, May 12, 2015. https://www.pewforum.org/2015/05/12/americas-changing-religious-landscape/.

———. "What Surveys Say about Worship Attendance and Why Some Stay Home." Pew, September 13, 2013. https://www.pewresearch.org/fact-tank/2013/09/13/what-surveys-say-about-worship-attendance-and-why-some-stay-home/.

Postman, Neil. *Amusing Ourselves to Death: Public Discourse in the Age of Show Business*. New York: Penguin, 2005.

Root, Andrew. *Faith Formation in a Secular Age*. Grand Rapids: Baker Academic, 2017.

———. *The Pastor in a Secular Age*. Grand Rapids: Baker Academic, 2019.

Smith, Christian, and Melina Lundquist Denton. *Soul Searching: The Religious and Spiritual Lives of American Teenagers*. New York: Oxford University Press, 2009.

Smith, James K. A. *Desiring the Kingdom*. Grand Rapids: Baker Academic, 2009.

Stewart, Matthew. *Nature's God: The Heretical Origins of the American Republic*. New York: Norton, 2014.

Stone, Bryan. *Evangelism After Pluralism: The Ethics of Christian Witness*. Grand Rapids: Baker Academic, 2018.

———. *Evangelism After Christendom: The Theology and Practice of Christian Witness*. Grand Rapids: Brazos, 2007.

Taylor, Charles. *A Secular Age*. Cambridge, MA: Belknap of Harvard University Press, 2018.

Wright, N.T. *Surprised By Hope: Rethinking Heaven, the Resurrection, and the Mission of the Church*. New York: HarperOne, 2018.

Yoder, John Howard. *The Politics of Jesus*. Grand Rapids: Eerdmans, 1994.